"Keir Weimer is an inspiring comeback story. He learned your chance to allow him to help you change yours."

—RORY VADEN
New York Times Bestselling Author of Take the Stairs and Hall of Fame Keynote Speaker

"Keir's insights are practical, valuable, and 'real world' ready. Take 5 minutes to try one of the tips or strategies featured in the book and see for yourself!"

—JARED KLEINERT
TED Speaker, Award-Winning Author, and USA Today's "Most Connected Millennial"

"We are all products of our past experiences, successes, and failures. Each of us has to decide whether we are victims or victors. Keir Weimer has laid his past bare and provides practical wisdom for living an inspired life. This book will help you grow as a person and become a victor."

—ADAM WEITSMAN,
CEO, Upstate Shredding

"***Live Inspired!*** is a wonderful outcome of Keir's story and, more importantly, his resilience. He blends his lessons learned, and from them offers powerful principles to practice. A great read for all of us committed to growth and moving from just living to being ALIVE."

—DANNY BADER,
Bestselling Author of Back From Heaven's Front Porch, Abraham's Diner, and I Met Jesus for a Miller Lite

"Keir's story is powerful and he has generously opened up about his difficult past. He shows he can guide thousands to their own freedom and a better life. This book will change lives."

—NICK ONKEN,
Celebrity Photographer & Podcast host

"This book will help you live more intentionally, more fully, and grow as a person and a professional. I highly recommend it!"

—ANTON J. GUNN,
Leadership Consultant

"***Live Inspired!*** traces the steps of a journey that no one wants to take. We don't get to choose what happens in life, but we can choose how we respond. Keir has chosen to grow in compassion and wisdom as a result, and we can all learn from his response."

—LISA FEY,
Global Speaker and Business Communication Author

"Keir Weimer's successes were built on a foundation of resilience and unwavering vision. Distilling his triumphs over adversity down to strategic bits of wisdom and easy-to-replicate behaviors, ***Live Inspired!*** is sure to help readers achieve results."

—HILARY BILLINGS,
Keynote Speaker and On-camera Host at Red Carpet Confidence

LIVE INSPIRED!

5-Minute Intentions to Energize Your Life and Career

Keir Weimer

FREEDOM INTERNATIONAL
PRESS

FREEDOM INTERNATIONAL
PRESS

Published by Freedom International Press

Created in collaboration with StoryBuilders (MyStoryBuilders.com)

ISBN: 978-1-7342539-0-0

First edition
Printed in the United States of America

To my late father, Mark Weimer, my best friend, mentor and the wisest man I've ever known. My dad taught me about life—about what's truly important—and about the value of the most precious resource to be treasured above all else in this world: our time.

This book, my life's work, and my love are dedicated to both you, Dad, and to you, Mom. Thank you for always believing in me, for never giving up on me and for everything you both have done for me. I love each of you more every day.

CONTENTS

INTRODUCTION

IF YOU'RE READING this book, you're likely someone who values personal growth and wants to take your career, your relationships and your life to a new level. If so, you're in the right place!

I'm excited you're joining me on this journey of growth, exploration, introspection and self-reflection to learn ways to be more inspired and intentional in all areas of your life.

If you've ever felt discouraged, lacking clarity and generally not living an inspired life, then this book is for you. Because I believe we all deserve and have the opportunity, once we give ourselves permission, to live inspired each and every day! I believe we all want, deep down, to be able to show up for life with enthusiasm—to be intentional in our actions and fully present.

When we live every day intentionally, we can truly live a more purposeful life. That's what this book will help you do. With short, intentional readings in subjects ranging from leadership and mindset, to purpose and relationships, I draw on my life experience to share lessons and principles that have helped me achieve things beyond what I ever thought imaginable.

Like you, I also highly value personal growth and education. I invest a lot of time, money and attention into finding new ways to become a better person, entrepreneur and leader.

Before we get started, I want to take a few moments and tell you a little bit about my background. My story is one of extreme tragedy, reinvention and redemption. Before I became a successful entrepreneur, I spent almost four years in prison as a result of an accident I caused that claimed the life of my college friend. The experience galvanized my determination to live a life of purpose and to find a way to make a positive impact in this world.

I realized the way I was living was preventing me from realizing my vision and dreams. Through developing an extreme commitment to my vision, I've been able to persevere through numerous obstacles to overcome discouragement and achieve true freedom in life, so I can live a life of purpose and impact—on my terms—in the service of others. I've been fortunate to be able to build purpose, wealth, happiness, and impact over my young professional career through several businesses I have founded and grown. At this point in my growth, I'm now most excited and focused on helping others grow and create a life on their terms, as well.

While contemplating the events that led up to me sitting in a cold prison cell, I realized my first step was to accept responsibility for the tragic accident I had caused. I decided then at age twenty-four that I would not only learn from my mistakes, but take action. I chose to change my life to find redemption, to become sober and live a sober life, and to contribute to the success of others.

Starting over again at age twenty-eight when I was released from prison, I promised myself that in spite of having no job, no driver's license, no money, being on parole and living at home with a curfew, I would never give up.

I faced many more challenges following my release, most notably being denied by all the graduate schools I applied to. I made the decision to be an entrepreneur and take control of my life and my fate. I decided to create a massive vision for my life with well-defined goals. The challenging process required a relentless commitment to my end vision but with flexibility on the means. I also needed to persevere to overcome the challenges and the discouragement I encountered in order to grow and rise.

My purpose in writing this book is to help you live a better, more mindful and inspired life, so that you too can elevate your career, enrich your relationships, reach new levels of success and achieve your true potential in all areas of life.

I am merely a humble observer of the world, although a focused practitioner in my various entrepreneurial ventures. What I will be sharing here in this book, are the lessons, the insights, the strategies and the various philosophies on life, career, business, relationships and other areas that I have developed through my journey. It is also a function of the people and the wisdom, the interactions and the teachings, that have informed me and my experience in this world.

I'm a firm believer in the concept of contribution and paying forward what we learn and achieve in this world to help others. I've distilled much of my life's philosophy and journey into the short readings that follow. I hope you'll find my perspective on personal and professional development to be of value and implement the tactical tips and strategies and in your life to achieve results. I hope this book will energize your life and inspire your success!

I have grouped these short, inspirational readings into sections that build upon one another as you grow. They are designed to be read in order, but you could just as easily select any single one and derive value from it at any time and jump around if you'd like. You could use it as a sort of reference guide for inspiration and perspective in the various subject matter areas.

I also want to take a moment to explain the format and structure of the book so you can get the most out of it. Each short reading concludes with four points:

 ## POWER QUOTE

A strong and sticky quotation from a key thought leader to accent the main message from the reading.

 ## KEY INSIGHT

The fundamental or critical take away that you can leverage to create a breakthrough in your life.

 ## TACTICAL TIP

A tactical piece of advice you can act on right away and implement into your personal or professional life to see results.

 ## DAY CHECK

An accountability tool to circle back at the end of your day to see how well you acted and implemented the lesson from the reading for that day.

I kept the readings short so you can engage with them easily and quickly and provided the four points to help make them actionable for you. I really want you to be empowered to implement the lessons and insights from each reading so you can see results in your life, like I have in mine.

I also hope you'll consider regularly engaging with the readings in the morning. My morning routine is absolutely critical to my success. I believe if you want to take control of your life, you have to take control of your morning and your day first. As you master each morning, and conquer each day, you'll begin to take charge of your life a little more each day.

My massive vision and goal with this book and my life's work, is to see 100 million+ people living an Inspired Life, achieving their goals and vision, and creating true freedom and a life on their terms—starting with you!

Now...

Let's GO!

To your success and happiness in life,

Keir Weimer

———

PART ONE

PURPOSE

*You can't achieve your potential
until you know your purpose.*

P URPOSE IS SO important to living fully and completely in this world. Many people go through life without ever
taking the time to really think deeply about what their true
purpose is in life and then create and live a life in congruence
with it.

It's important to ask the tough questions, do the complex inner
work, face our fears, fail and learn before we rise and succeed.

Purpose for me is everything in life. Unfortunately in my experience on earth, it took me twenty-three years and a horrible
tragedy to learn my true purpose in life. I was responsible for
an alcohol-related boat accident in my senior year of college
that claimed the life of my friend and subsequently sent me to
prison for three and a half years.

After being in prison for a year, away from my family and my
life, having gone through intensive substance abuse and alcohol treatment, I finally came to the realization of my true
purpose after getting really honest and transparent. I had to
forgive myself for what I had done and take full responsibility
for my life and my destiny moving forward.

I realized in that moment that I had a unique opportunity and
choice in front of me: I chose not to let this terrible tragedy
claim two lives. I have a duty to my friend's memory and legacy, and a duty to my goals and ambitions, to make an impact
in this world, to pay my message forward. I have a duty to live

a productive life as a contributing member of society and do everything I can to improve and help others do the same. Each and every day, I'm fortunate to be alive on this earth.

In that moment of decision in prison, I realized my purpose was to positively impact as many people as I possibly could. The future was unclear, but my purpose was crystal clear.

I would later come to attempt this through building companies, movements and brands that have gained the power and influence to change lives for the better. I knew that my purpose was not to be quiet about what happened, but rather to share it with the world in hopes of helping others avoid similar accidents and circumstances in their own figurative prisons.

I knew I had a chance to lead and take all that I have learned to inspire others to break free from their limiting beliefs and circumstances, so they can step into their greatness, achieve freedom and abundance in life, and create and live life on their own terms.

That is my purpose, and that is what purpose means to me, which is why it is the first section in this book.

GET THE FREE DOWNLOAD—*7 Frameworks to Live an Inspired Life*—at *LiveInspiredBook.com*

THE POWER OF WHY

WE'RE OFTEN CONFRONTED with thoughts and ideas of what we want in life.

- *What are our goals?*
- *What do we need to do to get there?*
- *How can others help us or give us the steps to take?*
- *Where can we find the support and encouragement to get there?*

This is all great and even important.

But it fails to identify the essence, to penetrate to the core and get at the driving question that can open up a world of opportunity for personal and professional growth:

- *WHY?*
- *Why do we do the things we do?*
- *Why do we get up at 5 a.m. when other people sleep in?*
- *Why do we do the hard things others won't?*
- *Why do we work as hard as we do, make sacrifices, work long hours, tirelessly build our businesses and improve our lives?*

You might ask, *Why must we start with WHY? Why is WHY so important? If I know What I do and How to do it, can't I get to where I want to go?*

Maybe.

But you might take much longer and arrive at the destination alone.

The driving motivation of the world's most effective and successful leaders is a force that's hard to describe, but easy to be attracted to and inspired by—WHY.

- *Why was Michael Jordan so driven to be the best basketball player of his time, and arguably ever?*

Michael Jordan wasn't massively successful and inspirational because of his field goal percentage or because he practiced his shots from the field longer than anyone else in practice.

- *Why was Steve Jobs so committed to his vision and what was his WHY?*

Steve Jobs and Apple weren't massively successful because their iPhone had the most features and the coolest design. In fact, other phones were often faster and larger with more features.

- *Why has Mark Zuckerberg been so wildly successful in pioneering an entire industry now ubiquitously known as social media? He wasn't driven by money and fame; we've seen him balk at both.*

Zuckerberg and Facebook haven't been so successful because they offer the most features and have taken the most traditional road to becoming a public company and social goliath.

For these leaders and so many others, success is not attributable to the *What* or the *How*.

What sets these leaders and visionaries apart from all the others, is that they all started with WHY.

And so must you.

Have an amazing day, seize every moment, don't waste a minute and be grateful for every opportunity to pursue and achieve your WHY!

LET'S GO!

POWER QUOTE

"Before we can stand out, we must first get clear on what we stand for."

—SIMON SINEK

KEY INSIGHT

The driving motivation of the world's most effective and successful leaders is a force that's hard to describe but easy to be attracted to and inspired by—WHY.

TACTICAL TIP

As you go about your day today, think about WHY you do what you do.

 ## DAY CHECK

What insight did you gain today about WHY you do what you do?

YOUR FOCUS

STARTING WITH WHY should be the focus. It's not easy, nor is it natural.

Starting each of our days, our weeks, or our years with the focus on WHY will allow us to stay closely united with the purpose of our journey in this world—WHY we are here.

If WHY is our focus, a myriad of positive changes will be realized by ourselves and those around us.

We will naturally start to become more passionate, clear and purposeful.

Our intentions will become more deliberate.

Congruence and authenticity will rise.

This is what is most noticeable and what I've realized happens in my life.

When I start with WHY, others place trust in me, are genuinely interested in my WHY and often want to be a part of the WHY.

When this happens, it's truly special and transformative—it marks the beginning of a team. Simon Sinek, author of *Start with Why*, puts it this way:

> *We can only provide a rational basis for a decision, when we can only point to tangible elements or rational measurements, the highest level of confidence we can give is, "I think this is the right decision."*
>
> *When we make gut decisions, the highest level of confidence we can offer is, "The decision feels right," even if it flies in the face of all the facts and figures.*
>
> *Again, this is biologically accurate, because gut decisions happen in the part of the brain that controls our emotions, not language.*
>
> *Ask the most successful entrepreneurs and leaders what their secret is, and invariably they all say the same thing: "I trust my gut."*
>
> *The times things went wrong, they will tell you, "I listened to what others were telling me, even though it didn't feel right. I should have trusted my gut."*
>
> *The ability to put a WHY into words provides the emotional context for decisions. It offers greater confidence than "I think it's right." It's more scalable than "I feel it's right."*
>
> *When you know your WHY, the highest level of confidence you can offer is, "I know it's right."*

When you know the decision is right, not only does it feel right, but you can also rationalize it and easily put it into words. The decision is fully balanced.

Sinek describes times when he would turn away business because a client didn't "feel right."

Personally, I've done this several times.

I will only work with clients that understand and buy into my team's WHY.

No longer will I take overpriced listings from demanding clients who think agents are commodities.

I work with those that believe in me and my team—and most importantly, our WHY.

When we focus in that way, we build trust.

Everything always comes back to trust—in business and in life.

LET'S GO!

 POWER QUOTE

"What do you focus on most often? What's your life's obsession? Finding love? Making a difference? Learning? Earning? Pleasing everyone? Avoiding pain? Changing the world? Are you aware of what you focus on most; your primary question in life? Whatever it is, it will shape, mold and direct your life."

—TONY ROBBINS

 ## KEY INSIGHT

The ability to put a WHY into words provides the emotional context for decisions.

 ## TACTICAL TIP

Pay attention to how you feel when you interact with others and what that might say about your WHY.

 ## DAY CHECK

What did you discover about your WHY as you monitored your feelings in your interactions today?

VISION

WE ARE ALL on a journey in this life. We go through it with one constant and common denominator.

We all have the same amount of time each day.

Therefore, it's up to us to use that time in the most productive, inspiring, enriching and achieving way.

Unfortunately, most people are held back from achieving their highest self, their greatest capacity for realizing a dream life on their terms.

The thing that holds most people back is a way of thinking that has been conditioned and adopted over time.

This is *not* something external.

It's *not* a force or a set of circumstances.

It's *not* someone else.

It's *not* another person's actions, opinions, or attitudes toward us or our lives.

It's *not* a government or an economy.

It's *not* a condition, function of a bank account, a skill set, or the lack of a skill set.

None of those things hold us back.

The only thing that holds people back from fully realizing what they dream and envision in life—is themselves.

It's you. It's me. It's all of us.

When we realize that the only thing holding us back from achieving our dreams and our wildest vision is ourselves—*then the world opens up for us.*

We need to take 100% accountability and responsibility and realize that the only way we will achieve this dream life is to realize the only person that is going to get us there is ourselves.

This is the hardest part for most people.

We are inhibited by the fears and false constructions that are in our minds.

They prevent us from realizing our dreams.

Most often, it is not external factors. Surroundings, upbringing, circumstances and access to certain privileges do not provide a higher likelihood of achieving success.

These factors make a difference for sure, but where the breakthrough happens is when we take ownership of our lives and the vision for our lives.

When we *focus* on us.

So I want to ask you to invest some time later today doing an exercise that will literally transform your life.

Write down who you want to become and how your life looks in the future.

This is called crafting and creating a Future Self.

Jot down the answers to these questions:

- *What you are wearing?*
- *Where you are physically located?*
- *What do you look like?*
- *Who are your friends?*
- *How much money do you have in your bank account in liquid funds?*
- *What do you have by way of investments and income streams?*
- *How many homes do you own?*
- *What you are doing for a living?*
- *Have you diversified your financial portfolio?*
- *What organizations are you a part of that provide meaning and purpose in your life?*
- *What community and tribe have you formed that looks up to you for leadership, guidance and wisdom?*
- *What legacy have you left for your family and for those you love and care about?*

In short, what do your future self and your future impact on the world look like?

Use descriptive, detailed words.

Take the time to invest in this and provide details about your vision for your future self and life.

After you've put this down on paper, post it where you can see it daily.

Now that you have brought these goals to the subconscious level and are being reminded daily of your future life, watch as your body, mind, internal faculties and external resources start to focus and move you closer and closer to achieving your future self and life.

We all desire to grow, to go from where we are today, to where we want to be in the future.

Start with this vision exercise to start bringing it to reality.

LET'S GO!

 ## POWER QUOTE

"Vision without action is merely a dream. Action without vision just passes the time. Vision with action can change the world."

—JOEL A. BAKER

KEY INSIGHT

The only thing that holds people back in life from realizing what they dream and envision—is themselves.

 ## TACTICAL TIP

Jot down what you want your Future Self to look like. As you go about your day, think about your decisions with this mindset: Will this further my Future Self goals?

 ## DAY CHECK

What did you do differently today as a result of your focused, Future Self mindset?

YOUR ONE THING

TODAY IS A new dawn in the growth of each and every one of us.

This is literally Day One.

Today.

Day One of a new week, a new month, a new year and Day One of the rest of your life.

Are you ready to treat it that way?

I'm talking about taking things to a completely different level. I'm talking about dreaming, conceiving and acting in a way so grand that it scares you.

Something so big that it seems impossible. So outsized, that it feels unattainable. I spent some time recently thinking about...

- *My goals and vision.*
- *New businesses I'm launching.*
- *My brand.*
- *My identity.*
- *My core values.*

What did I conclude?

That this is an absolutely amazing and unparalleled time to be alive and pursue a life of our wildest dreams!

We cannot take one moment of it for granted!

Take a moment and think about where you are in life right now. Then think about where you want to go in life.

Think about the largest life you can possibly conceive. Push the boundaries of what you think is even possible or realistic.

Put a multiple that seems crazy on what income you want to earn, maybe ten times what you're earning now.

Think about how you want your family to be, your schedule, your vacations, your... *everything!*

Dream big—really, really big—because there's no other way. You only get one chance to do this. I want you to see yourself living this life—this dream becoming a reality.

Now that you have a massive vision for your ideal life, you need a plan and action to bring it into reality and make it your life.

To break down what might seem like an overwhelming plan and strategy, you need to have a laser-like focus.

You need to find the ONE thing that will move the needle, set up a domino effect and propel you toward creating the energy and momentum needed to make this vision a reality.

As Gary Keller so famously said, we need to go small first in order to go big. So, I urge you to take fifteen minutes and focus on the single most important action or habit that will create unstoppable momentum toward your extraordinary vision for your ideal life.

Identify this action or habit. Schedule it. Time block it. Protect it over all else—and make sure it is *the* priority to start each day.

LET'S GO!

 ## POWER QUOTE

"You'll never change your life until you change something you do daily. The secret of your success is found in your daily routine."

—JOHN C. MAXWELL

 ## KEY INSIGHT

This is literally Day One. Today. Day One of a new week, a new month, a new year and Day One of the rest of your life.

 ## TACTICAL TIP

Identify one habit that, if you did it consistently and daily, would move the needle and help you achieve your ideal life.

DAY CHECK

What did you put in place today to help you keep the one thing front and center for you going forward?

YOUR SUPERPOWER

THE CHARACTER DIAMOND[1] test is used to dig deeper into your psyche and identity as a person.

The purpose is to help you get a better understanding of your fears, insecurities, weaknesses and tendencies.

After understanding these things, you can conquer them—and then turn your attention to your strengths and how to build your power as a person. The Character Diamond consists of four points:

- *Your Kryptonite: the number-one thing that takes you down*

- *The Hill You're Prepared to Die On: the number-one value you stand for, no matter what*

- *Your Flaws and Masks: things that get in the way of you showing up as the best version of yourself*

- *The North Star: it's who you innately are*

I want to focus on the last point: the North Star, your unique strength.

---

[1]   David S. Freeman, "Character Diamond", *Beyond Structure Master Class*, https://beyondstructure.com/.

For me, my superpower is my Extreme Commitment.

Extreme Commitment to my life, goals, ambitions, making a huge and lasting impact on the world and leaving a legacy I can be proud of.

I am determined and committed to my vision for a massive life of accomplishment, impact, contribution, fulfillment and success. I encourage you to dig deep and identify what your North Star is—*what is your superpower?*

If you don't know how to necessarily identify it, you can start by asking some questions and finding the answers to help you arrive at your core beliefs.

Everything stems and becomes apparent from there. What are your

- *Values?*
- *Drivers?*
- *Superpower traits?*
- *Innate characteristics?*

When I did this exercise, I listed some of my beliefs that then helped me arrive at my superpower.

I believe that....

- *Everyone deserves to live the life of their dreams, achieve happiness and success.*
- *Everyone deserves a second chance at life.*
- *Your past does not define or equal your future.*

- *We must confront our fears and the skeletons in our closet to become free.*
- *Always work toward living at peak state, highest and best self.*
- *You can always rewrite your story.*
- *Every day is Day One, and the first day of the rest of your life.*

What are some of your core beliefs that drive you as a person?

What is your North Star—your superpower—who you innately are as a talented, gifted, agent of change in the world?

LET'S GO!

 POWER QUOTE

"Your talent, plus passion, plus action, equals your super-power."

—NADALIE BARDO

 KEY INSIGHT

When you can understand your weaknesses, you can account for them and compensate with your strengths.

TACTICAL TIP

Think through your core beliefs. What do they tell you about who you are at the core?

 ## DAY CHECK

Where did you see evidence of your superpower strengths show up today?

WHO ARE YOU?

IDENTITY. THE DICTIONARY defines *identity* as the distinguishing character or personality of an individual.

Yet so many different things go into establishing and defining each of our unique identities.

It's a lifelong manifestation of our thoughts, beliefs, values, goals, words and the consistent accumulation of our actions and experiences. I think a lot of people, especially in our society today, strive for an identity that might not be consistent with who they truly are.

There's so much societal pressure growing up, at home, in school, in peer groups and everywhere else in the media that pushes us to act a certain way.

Just think of how many friends and people you know who might have achieved outward success as defined by society, parents, or friends, but are not really happy or inspired as individuals?

I know so many people like this.

What does it even mean to be successful?

I think we need to define success and who we are as individuals, and not let the world define it for us.

For me personally, I think success is reaching a point where you are able to do what you love on your terms and know exactly why you are there.

When you know your purpose in the world, you can deliver that value and serve humanity in an intentional way each day.

When you reach this station in life and are good at what you do, all of the wealth, accolades, health and outward trappings of success will flow to you as a result—not as a cause.

We need to realize that each of us has a unique ability to deliver our experience and values to the world once we embrace our individual identity and push that energy out to the universe.

Each and every one of us has a chance to do amazing things here on this earth.

We serve others to impact people we engage with daily and leave a legacy of service and influence.

So, let's make sure we have fun today, dress up, get out there, choose an identity and enjoy ourselves in this life that we influence.

Let's make sure that we are proud and being true to our self and our identity in the way in which we show up and serve the world each day.

Here's a quote that I find to be very powerful for you to ponder today:

Keep your thoughts positive because your thoughts become your words.

Keep your words positive because your words become your behavior.

Keep your behavior positive because your behavior becomes your habits.

Keep your habits positive because your habits become your values.

Keep your values positive because your values become your destiny.

—MAHATMA GANDHI

LET'S GO!

 POWER QUOTE

"The world is full of people that are going to tell you who you are, but that's for you to decide."

—AUNT LUCY

KEY INSIGHT

When you know your purpose in the world, you can deliver that value and serve humanity in an intentional way each day.

 ## TACTICAL TIP

Identify one thing that defines success for you and commit to not letting the world define it for you.

 ## DAY CHECK

What one thing did you identify about your purpose today and what pressures did you face to let others define it for you?

ARE YOU A LIFELONG LEARNER?

EDUCATION, PERSONAL ENRICHMENT and becoming a lifelong learner and student of the world—these are critical to your success. These are values my parents instilled in me at an early age.

From a young age, I always enjoyed writing, exploring and learning new things.

I excelled at school, always challenged myself with coursework and made a point to travel the world.

I started this pursuit of knowledge and culture at an early age.

I owe most of this to my parents, who instilled in me the importance of education and learning and investing time and energy into improving your mind.

I wasn't always the most prolific reader, mainly because I was and still am restless, always on the go with a low attention span—and highly energetic.

These traits are great for being a motivated and determined business person but make it difficult to be a natural reader. I'm not someone who can easily sit for long periods of time.

I had to invest time into becoming a better reader, which I have done—especially more recently.

I started a book club with some friends.

I devote time in the morning and evening to reading. I read for enrichment and development to improve myself.

I do this for many reasons, but fundamentally I do this because of an innate and basic need to always be growing, always learning, always improving.

I strive to be better than the person I was yesterday—stronger, more mature and a better version of myself today in every sense as a result of what I learned yesterday. Why do I do this?

Because my WHY is *greatness*.

If we are not moving forward, growing, advancing and progressing in every area of life—then we are declining.

There is no status quo, no even keel, no treading water in life.

The universe is in constant flux. Every form of life and energy is either growing or waning. Businesses, personal fortunes, family power, health, nations and their power and place in the world—it's all always rising or falling, one or the other.

High achievers and the world's most successful people—whether in business, sports, politics or the arts—are committed to continual improvement.

If you want to be more successful, you need to learn to ask yourself:

- *How can I make this better?*
- *How can I innovate?*
- *How can I step out of my zone of comfort and familiarity?*
- *How can I learn more about this, be better than the next invention or competitor?*
- *How can I provide more value to more people?*

Are you committed to a life of constant learning, improvement, advancement?

Are you ready to always strive for and achieve greatness in all you endeavor to accomplish in life?

Are you ready to push the boundaries of what you thought was conceivable and achievable, and live the life of your dreams?

Are you a lifelong learner?

LET'S GO!

 ## POWER QUOTE

"Change is the law of life. And those who look only to the past or present are certain to miss the future."

—JOHN F. KENNEDY

 ## KEY INSIGHT

There is no status quo, no even keel, no treading water in life. The universe is in constant flux. Every form of life and energy is either growing or waning.

 ## TACTICAL TIP

Choose one thing you will do today to improve yourself and learn something you never knew before.

 ## DAY CHECK

In what ways today did your commitment to advance in life shine through? In what ways today did you push forward and better yourself for the future.

INTENTION 8

CORE COMPETENCY

NOW THAT YOU'VE identified WHY you are driven in life, let's talk about the WHAT—your unique genius or core competency.

The best way to fortune, high achievement, accolades, greatness and sincere contentment in life is *not* through pursuing those very things.

No. Those who pursue and are driven by those things as their WHY often fail and never attain them.

Success in life and in business follows those who do what they are best at doing, what they want to do and what they do with passion.

Period.

The biggest mistake people make in life is not trying to make a living at doing what they most enjoy.

Greer Garson put it this way: "Starting out to make money is the greatest mistake in life. Do what you feel you have a flair for doing, and if you are good enough at it, the money will come."

It's so critical to decide and find out what you really, really love to do, and what you're also really good at—then delegate *everything* else.

Complete delegation. You assign, train and set standards for tasks—and then let it go.

Focus on your core competencies and what you get passionate about—and nothing more. Successful entrepreneurs get other people to pay them to practice getting better at what they love to do.

Steven Spielberg loves to make movies. People pay him big money to make movies.

Every time he works on a film, he learns more about directing, producing and filmmaking.

He gets to practice and hang out with other filmmakers, all while getting paid for it.

Elon Musk is one of the greatest visionaries and entrepreneurs of our generation, changing entire industries and the way we look at the world.

He's not driven by money. He's driven to change the world and leave a mark.

He's a billionaire many times over as a result of getting paid for his passion.

Whatever it is for you, make sure you are doing what you are best at in life.

Find what you truly enjoy doing. Do your true passion.

Find what keeps you up at night as you think about it.

What moves you to greatness?

What keeps the itch and urge to succeed alive and healthy?

When you find this, embrace it with everything you have and give it 150%—and then never look back.

All of the rest will fall into place, mark my words.

LET'S GO!

 ## POWER QUOTE

"Do what you love, the money will follow."

—MALCOLM S. FORBES

 ## KEY INSIGHT

Focus on your core competencies and what you get passionate about—and nothing more.

TACTICAL TIP

List things you love to do. Then list the things you are good at. Find the connections. What can you delegate to find more time to focus on your core competency?

 ## DAY CHECK

What did you choose to delegate today so you could focus on your core competency?

PART TWO

MINDSET

Your life and your success are
only limited by your mindset.

I THINK IF WE had to boil down what really separates those who achieve greatness and success in life—however you choose to define those two things—it would be the mindset that these people have developed. I'm a firm believer that you can truly achieve anything in this world you put your mind to. If you develop the courage and the strength of character and mind to set the intention, build a plan and strategy, and marshall the resources, people and skills, you can achieve anything your mind intends.

You must then commit relentlessly to your vision while being flexible on your methods and the *how*, and persevere no matter the challenges or obstacles that arise on your journey to achieve your vision and goals in life.

The fact of the matter is that the mind is our framework for existence, and the larger we expand our framework for thought and achievement, the more we will think bigger and achieve greater in this world.

For me, I developed my ironclad mindset to achieve greatness and success in life through my experience and time dealing with the tragedy I caused. My time spent in prison, which is one of the most difficult places in the world to live and exist, was an environment where it is hard to survive, let alone thrive.

I accepted responsibility, forgave myself and found peace and purpose within. As a result, being sent to prison became a gift, the best thing that ever happened to me. I stay committed to my life of sobriety and to my master vision and purpose in this world by remembering my friend, her legacy. I strive to ensure my actions align with paying respect to that and appreciating the sheer opportunity I have to even be alive at any one moment.

I also gain strength and courage to persevere through many obstacles by keeping my ambition and my purpose front and center at all times to live a massive life of contribution and to help and contribute to others in this world.

GET THE FREE DOWNLOAD—*7 Frameworks to Live an Inspired Life—at LiveInspiredBook.com*

WHAT SCARES YOU?

WHATEVER SCARES YOU, gives you anxiety, makes you feel uneasy, nervous, or uncomfortable in life—identify what that is—and introduce more of it into your life.

Immediately!

That's why you are reading this book, isn't it?

Are you looking to achieve exponential growth in your personal life, in your professional life, in your businesses and beyond? That requires you to stretch in a lot of areas and often become quite uncomfortable. We need to create life experiences that force us to stretch. We must stretch to grow. Like a muscle, if we don't push and stretch, we won't grow ourselves and our lives. I'm a huge fan of personal and professional development.

I invest a lot of time, money and energy into growing and learning in every way I can: books, podcasts, coaching, conferences, retreats, masterminds, courses—you name it. I push myself with new experiences and meeting interesting people every day.

I'm also constantly trying to identify lingering fears and face them head-on.

I recently went to a conference where I became super honest and vulnerable with myself and with hundreds of strangers. I shared a very personal story of my life.

The catch? I had to share my story in three minutes. Only 3 minutes!

For someone who is naturally verbose and long-winded, who never wrote an essay in school or college under the word limit, who always goes over the allotted time—this was extremely challenging for me, given the sheer volume of content and the personal nature of it.

However, I quickly jumped at this opportunity to deliver my message in this highly-condensed format—because I knew it would challenge me and push me outside my comfort zone.

I knew it would force me to make sacrifices and cut to the very core of my message and story. I knew there was pressure and no turning back once I signed up. It would be a sort of a Cortés-like "burning of the ships" moment.

I *had* to be ready.

I *had* to find a way.

I *had* to overcome the anxiety and slight fear, and deliver. Make sure you find ways to stretch each and every day.

Do things that scare you, big and small.

Book things to do where others are watching.

Set wild goals like exercising every day for the rest of the year, when you usually go to the gym once a week.

Whatever it is, make sure you're always looking to stretch beyond your comfort zone and into the areas of fear and anxiety.

That is where genuine growth in mind, body, spirit and life experience truly happens. Have an awesome day!

LET'S GO!

 POWER QUOTE

"In any given moment we have two options: to step forward into growth or step back into safety."

—ABRAHAM MASLOW

 KEY INSIGHT

Whatever scares you, gives you anxiety, makes you feel uneasy, nervous, or uncomfortable in life—identify what that is—and introduce more of it into your life.

 TACTICAL TIP

What challenge has you a little afraid today? What are you anxious about? See if it represents a growth opportunity for you, and take the first step to embracing it today.

DAY CHECK

In what ways today did you stretch yourself to face your fears or insecurities? How will you continue to stretch yourself tomorrow?

YOUR THINKING STORY

THERE IS A direct connection between changing our poor thinking habits and living a more successful and happy life. *Thinking habits?*

Yes—the way we think, process information, interpret the world around us, make sense of it all and take action all come from "thinking habits" we've developed over the years.

These habits are mostly a function of our environment.

What if, however, our thinking habits are not good habits? For example, sometimes our eating habits are not healthy habits.

What if the way we view events around us, the way we perceive and process external things and internal emotions, is actually holding us back?

Think about this for a minute. As a real estate professional and luxury broker in one of my businesses, I'm in the business of marketing, whether I want to believe it or not. I would never get a chance to sell a property if I weren't first successful in marketing.

I've never shown a house without first getting a buyer interested. One precedes the other. But what is marketing, and what makes someone a good marketer?

I see marketing as the art of effective storytelling.

Creative storytelling can move someone from where they are to a place of desired and intended action. For example, from elicited interest to a closed sale in real estate. But what if we're telling the wrong stories? Not to buyers or clients—but to ourselves?

What if our thinking habits are, in fact, hurting us and holding us back from achieving our own true greatness?

What if these thinking habits are actually "errors in thinking"? This is a way of thinking and processing that doesn't truly work. It's an illogical and incorrect thought framework.

We live life through telling and consuming stories. We've always done so since the beginning of language—and even before that, through graphic depictions of life and experience.

What if you are telling yourself the wrong story of your life?

What if you are playing out a false narrative that is actually not your story?

What if you are holding yourself back by not believing enough in what could be, and in a huge vision for your ideal life—and instead you're telling yourself a false story?

What if that untrue story keeps you from pushing the envelope, going outside of your comfort area, prevents you from taking calculated risks and pursuing your passion?

What if one error in thinking was simply thinking you couldn't or shouldn't live the life of your dreams and your highest vision for you and those you love? But...

What if you stopped telling yourself a limiting story that prevented you from living and reaching your true potential and vision?

What would happen then?

The mind is the most beautiful and amazing thing. The energy and the momentum it can create, either positive or negative, and its effect on life...is simply extraordinary.

The amazing thing is that you have the ability to change how you are thinking in order to attract more positive energy and momentum into your life.

The most potent form of energy is thought, because thought-waves are cosmic waves penetrating all time and space.

As the saying goes... *"Watch your thoughts, they become words. Watch your words, they become actions. Watch your actions, they become habits. Watch your habits, they become your character. Watch your character, it becomes your destiny."* —UNKNOWN

Our thoughts can become and create our destiny!

Think about the power of your "Thinking Story"!

LET'S GO!

 ## POWER QUOTE

"A man is but the product of his thoughts—what he thinks, he becomes."

—GANDHI

 ## KEY INSIGHT

There is a direct connection between changing our poor thinking habits and living a more successful and happy life.

 ## TACTICAL TIP

Write down some of your thinking habits. Sort them into positive and negative. Which habits don't align with your positive outlook and goals and need to go? Which ones should you keep to help shape your new future?

 ## DAY CHECK

How did your mindset about your story affect your habits today? What bad habits appeared when you were struggling? What good habits surfaced when you were in a positive place?

———

FREEDOM

THERE IS A fundamental value that underpins everything I do and the way in which I have chosen to live my life.

That value is Freedom.

Freedom is the power or right to act, speak, or think as one wants without hindrance or restraint.

- *Freedom to live a life of our dreams and achieve happiness and success*

- *Freedom of thought and expression and creative ideas*

- *Freedom of, and independence over, how we choose to live our lives, create our schedule, travel, pursue ideas and businesses that we love*

- *Freedom to earn what we want by announcing to the world this is our value, and then having the ability to back it up*

I live in such an amazing country with freedoms. I hope you do, too. We all live in such an unprecedented time. Yet we often tell ourselves stories that hold us back from living in freedom. But what if we were telling the wrong stories, limiting stories driven by fear?

We don't need to anymore. No one needs to—including you.

I've been investing time developing my philosophy on life and program for living a life of freedom in every area.

I am so incredibly excited about being able to help people all over the world break free from their fears or limiting stories and find the strength to create and live the life of their dreams on their own terms.

What about you? Will you realize the power we all have to escape constrictions, fears, our painful pasts, bad relationships and the captivities of our minds?

Will you acknowledge that with a change in thinking, habits, health and mindset you can open an entirely new world of opportunity?

This positive attitude and life approach is also arguably one of the fundamental ingredients for creating a truly great culture in an organization.

Positive energy, enthusiasm and a *joie de vivre* are contagious. They attract other people.

People want to be around people who are full of positive energy, exude confidence and peace of mind and have a strong and unwavering attitude in the face of adversity.

These are the traits of a true leader.

This is the positive mindset that makes for a really strong culture to attract the *right* people into your orbit who share your values and want to be a part of a story of freedom in every sense.

LET'S GO!

 ## POWER QUOTE

"You cannot have a positive life and a negative mind."

—JOYCE MEYER

 ## KEY INSIGHT

Will you realize the power we all have to escape constrictions, fears, our painful pasts, bad relationships and the captivities of our minds?

 ## TACTICAL TIP

Take a few minutes each day to write down some things you're thankful for. Look at what you wrote, and think about how much you have to be thankful for because of the freedoms you enjoy. This time of intentional thankfulness will get your mind into a positive mindset that shapes your day.

 ## DAY CHECK

How did you notice your positivity affecting or attracting others today? How did you use your freedom to choose and break away from negativity, fear or insecurity?

GO BOLD

I 'M IN A book club that I started. We read a book every month in the self-help/personal development genre and have a thirty-minute call and discussion about it once a week.

Our first book was one I chose—*Bold: How to Go Big, Create Wealth and Impact the World* written by Peter Diamandis and Steven Kotler.

The title alone really resonated with me. One of the key things the authors talk about is having a bold mindset—mindset is EVERYTHING! How can you change your perspective and mindset from a hesitant one of scarcity and doubt to a bold one of abundance and a winning mentality?

This is not always easy—it depends on where you come from, how you grew up and how you think about the world. It's an important and powerful concept, one that most people never quite understand.

I'm a firm believer in the power of mindset and visioning and have practiced it in my personal and professional life.

Laying the framework and creating the fertile mental playing field for big thought and goals is huge. Then creatively incubating it and having the confidence and commitment to execute is a massive achievement.

Goals small and big can benefit from this approach. I've seen it yield amazing results time and time again in my life. In *Bold*, the authors put it this way:

> *Big goals work best when there's an alignment between an individual's values and the desired outcome of the goal. When everything lines up, we're totally committed— meaning we're paying even more attention, are even more resilient, and are way more productive as a result.*
>
> *Organizational inertia comes from a fear of failure. This fear is the reason Kodak didn't recognize the brilliance of the digital camera, IBM initially dismissed the personal computer and America Online (AOL) is, well, barely online.*[2]

Autonomy is the desire to steer our own ship. Mastery is the desire to steer it well. Purpose is the need for the journey to mean something.

As you prepare to master today, consider the following "Creed of the Persistent and Passionate Mind" by Peter Diamandis:

1. If anything can go wrong, fix it! (To hell with Murphy!)
2. When given a choice—take both!
3. Multiple projects lead to multiple successes.
4. Start at the top, then work your way up.

---

[2] Peter Diamandis & Steven Kotler, *Bold: How to Go Big, Create Wealth and Impact the World* (Simon & Schuster, 2016), 120.

5. Do it by the book . . . but be the author!

6. When forced to compromise, ask for more.

7. If you can't win, change the rules.

8. If you can't change the rules, then ignore them.

9. Perfection is not optional.

10. When faced without a challenge—make one.

11. No simply means begin one level higher.

12. Don't walk when you can run.

13. When in doubt: THINK!

14. Patience is a virtue, but persistence to the point of success is a blessing.

15. The squeaky wheel gets replaced.

16. The faster you move, the slower time passes, the longer you live.

17. The best way to predict the future is to create it yourself!

18. The ratio of something to nothing is infinite.

19. You get what you incentivize.

20. If you think it is impossible, then it is for you.

21. An expert is someone who can tell you exactly how something can't be done.

22. The day before something is a breakthrough, it's a crazy idea.

23. If it was easy, it would have been done already.

24. Without a target, you'll miss it every time.

25. Fail early, fail often, fail forward!

26. If you can't measure it, you can't improve it.

27. The world's most precious resource is the persistent and passionate human mind.

28. Bureaucracy is an obstacle to be conquered with persistence, confidence and a bulldozer when necessary.

LET'S GO!

 ## POWER QUOTE

"Freedom lies in being bold."

—ROBERT FROST

 ## KEY INSIGHT

Autonomy is the desire to steer our own ship. Mastery is the desire to steer it well. Purpose is the need for the journey to mean something.

 ## TACTICAL TIP

Go bold! Pick an area in your life where you are comfortable and challenge yourself. Start small and build your new mindset by challenging your comfort zone.

DAY CHECK

In what way today did you challenge yourself and push boundaries by changing your mindset?

LIVING AT SCALE

ELON MUSK IS someone who I follow closely. He's been transformational to so many industries and businesses.

One of the first things we can learn from Musk's example is that he is relentless in his pursuit of the bold, and is totally unfazed by concerns about scaling success.

Elon was the founder of several early startups, including a little company called Paypal. He netted $100 million when he sold it.

He then set out to transform other industries. He formed SpaceX, SolarCity and Tesla, taking on space travel, sustainable transportation and solar energy as well. His companies are now worth several billion dollars. Elon has always thought at scale and never been intimidated by huge obstacles, entrenched industries and big setbacks.

When he couldn't get a job, he started a company. When internet commerce stalled, he reinvented banking.

When he couldn't find decent launch services for his Martian greenhouse, he went into the rocket business.

As a kicker, because he never lost interest in the problem of energy, he started both an electric car and a solar energy company. It is also worth pointing out that Tesla is the first successful car company that started in America in five decades and SolarCity has become one of the nation's largest residential solar providers.

All told, in slightly less than a dozen years, Musk's appetite for bold has created an empire worth about $30 billion.

So what's his secret?

Musk has a few, but none are more important to him than passion and purpose.

Here's how he put it:

> I didn't go into the rocket business, the car business, or the solar business thinking this is a great opportunity. I just thought, in order to make a difference, something needed to be done. I wanted to have an impact. I wanted to create something substantially better than what came before.[3]

Every entrepreneur is driven by passion and purpose. Why?

Passion and purpose scale easily—they are contagious and transferable—always have been, always will be.

Every movement, every revolution, is proof of this fact. Doing anything big and bold is difficult.

---

3   *ibid.*

Think of being awake at two in the morning for the fifth night in a row. You need to keep going. You need to fill yourself, but how?

You're only going to fuel yourself from deep within. You're not going to push ahead when it's someone else's mission. It needs to be yours.

Having passion and purpose is merely the first step.

> The usual life cycle of starting a company begins with a lot of optimism and enthusiasm. This lasts for about six months, and then reality sets in. That's when you learn a lot of your assumptions were false, and that the finish line is much farther away than you thought. It's during this period that most companies die rather than scale up.[4]

This is also where Musk urges direct and blunt feedback from close friends.

> "It's not going to be easy, but it's really important to solicit negative feedback from friends. In particular, feedback that helps you recognize as fast as possible what you're doing wrong and adjust course. That's usually what people don't do. They don't adjust course fast enough and adapt to the reality of the situation."

Musk employs a number of other strategies, including one he borrowed from physics.

---

[4]   *ibid.*

Physics training is a good framework for reasoning," explains Musk. "It forces you to boil things down to their most fundamental truths and then connect those truths in a way that lets you understand reality. This gives you a way to attack the counterintuitive, a way of figuring out things that aren't obvious. When you're trying to create a new product or service, I think it's critical to use this framework for reasoning. It takes a lot of mental energy, but it's still the right way to do it.[5]

Follow Musk's example and begin today to think—and live—at scale!

LET'S GO!

 POWER QUOTE

"A great leader's courage to fulfill his vision comes from passion, not position."

—JOHN C. MAXWELL

 KEY INSIGHT

In order to be bold, to be wildly successful and create a legacy—we need to go outside of our normal, our day-to-day, and think, operate and live "at scale."

---

[5]   *ibid.*

TACTICAL TIP

Check your passion level. Are you passionate about your job? If you are not passionate about it, you will not have the drive to do what needs to be done. You need a fuel inside to live at scale.

 ## DAY CHECK

Where did your passion give you the motivation to complete a task today? Where did your purpose or goal give you the inner fuel to complete a task?

HOW TO CREATE A BREAKTHROUGH

I THINK WE ALL are looking, to varying degrees, for a breakthrough of some sort.

We want an epiphany—a point in time where we can make the conscious decision to reject the status quo as we move forward.

To decide that where we are is not where we want to be.

We can achieve whatever we want if we have the capacity to dream, envision, create a plan *and* have the work ethic to achieve it. I attended a Tony Robbins' "Unleash the Power Within" conference and have been coaching with his organization.

I follow Robbins closely and really value his leadership and pioneering work in the field. So much so, that I want to share Tony's 3 steps to achieving a breakthrough:

1. CHANGE YOUR STRATEGY.

The best mindset can't overcome a bad plan. As Tony Robbins says:

Running east looking for a sunset, I don't care how posi-tive you are, I don't care how hard you work at it, it's not going to work, it's the wrong strategy.[6]

He suggests you find people who've achieved turnarounds and transformations and study what went right.

2. CHANGE YOUR STORY.

Common excuses like "I'm just not good at relationships" or "Only those born rich get richer" are the stories we tell our-selves that keep us from implementing our goals.

Robbins says we must divorce ourselves from stories that limit us in order to unlock our true potential.

3. CHANGE YOUR STATE.

If you're constantly stressed, overwhelmed or frustrated, you won't have the fuel to implement your goals. Instead, you'll develop a disempowering story, telling yourself that nothing can change and that nothing works.

Find a way to recharge.

Your mental and emotional state determines your perception of life and is essential to any breakthrough.

---

[6]   Tony Robbins, "How Firewalking Will Help You Achieve More Breakthroughs," *Tony Robbins Firewalker*, May 4, 2017, https://tonyrobbinsfirewalk.com/firewalking-will-help-achieve-breakthroughs/.

That's how you begin to create a breakthrough starting right now!

LET'S GO!

 ## POWER QUOTE

"Your life does not get better by chance, it gets better by change."

—JIM ROHN

 ## KEY INSIGHT

Breakthroughs come from a change in strategy, story, and state of mind.

 ## TACTICAL TIP

How do you tell your story? Is your mindset a negative or positive one? Self-reflection on your strategy, story and mindset will help you see changes you need to make.

 ## DAY CHECK

Where did you have a breakthrough today? What friction did you push past to win the day?

STAY TEACHABLE

I'VE GOTTEN REALLY deliberate about putting myself in positions where I am around people I can lean on, learn from, reach out to for help and find mentorship in new spaces and areas where I want to grow.

Seminars and events in which you are being mentored aren't just about what you get from the takeaways or the energy you get as you go home.

I'm learning more and more that these events are about the people that you meet and what you learn as you get outside your typical life experiences.

I'm talking about the value you get by stepping outside of your circle and your normal, predictable sphere.

You need to push yourself to grow into new areas of interest, talent or expertise. You need to pull the value from building community and relationships with new people in these environments and see what that can do for growth.

To that end, I'm learning how important it is to be humble in new pursuits and always remain—and be committed to—being a student of the craft.

Whatever your area of focus, business, skill, or expertise, you must remain teachable and willing to ask for help.

Leaning on others, both mentors and peers, is a valuable way to build camaraderie and community toward a shared goal.

We really gain strength by forming mutually beneficial relationships that support and give as well as receive.

There are events for all kinds of people from all over the world, so finding some for your interests won't be a problem.

People get together to help each other grow and strive to reach new heights in their business and in their lives, build new friendships and foster relationships that may continue far into the future.

You must be humble, teachable and remain in a state of perpetual self-improvement and development. You must be willing to invest in yourself and in your education, open to leaning on others for help and guidance.

Today I encourage and challenge you to do these things and see the benefits that can accrue and will manifest in your life as a result.

Watch the world open up for you and all that you seek to come within your reach.

LET'S GO!

POWER QUOTE

"For good ideas and true innovation, you need human interaction, conflict, argument, debate."

—MARGARET HEFFERNAN

KEY INSIGHT

Whatever your area of focus, business, skill, or expertise, you must remain teachable and willing to ask for help.

TACTICAL TIP

Try going out of your way to engage at least one new person today. Find at least one new setting or situation and interact to open the door to new relationships and opportunities for growth.

DAY CHECK

What did you learn from people you interacted with today? How did you feel about yourself after you made an interaction that produced a new insight for you?

LEANING IN

IF YOU WANT to move into new areas and transform to become the person you need to be for this next chapter of growth and level of play in life, you'll need to consider this principle.

One of the most important principles for growth is simply *leaning in* to a new pursuit or goal and surrendering to the will and the power of the process to get there.

What I mean by that is that as a Type A, highly driven and organized person, I want to have order, predictability and to plan and time everything.

However, life doesn't always follow a set plan or timeline. Sometimes when the most unique and profound transformation and growth happens, it's because we are simply open to it.

We organically lean into the process and surrender our will to the determination of the *how*, not necessarily the *why*, as that should be clear.

We often tell ourselves stories or think we should have something done a certain way, on a certain timeline and how it should be done to achieve our goal.

What I'm learning more and more, though, is that I am exactly where I need to be right now. Things shouldn't have happened any bit before or any bit after when it's happening right now, today, in this moment.

I'm so incredibly grateful for the people I am meeting—the energy, positivity, ambition and success that I'm around every day.

I am leaning in, making all of my intentions become reality by being fully present, open and surrendered to the process. As a result of doing this, I've had many opportunities I never would have imagined open right up.

Proximity is power.

We need to make sure we're strategically placing ourselves in the right circles, communities and around the right people we can network with, serve and help.

Find ways to elevate our own path.

That very concept is one of the most important things I've come to learn by attending a lot of events and Masterminds.

One of the most important benefits we can get by investing in our network growth and in building community through this method are the people that we become exposed to.

We learn their ideas and ways of thinking and how that knowledge can truly enrich and broaden our lives, moving us closer to where we want to ultimately be. Never stop dreaming big, reevaluating and being open and vulnerable to the fact that your dreams are going to change over time. The path to get there is going to shift multiple times.

And that's okay.

What we can really benefit from is leaning into the process and making sure that we're always open, receptive and ready to do what it takes to elevate and grow into that next version of our best selves.

Be ready to compete and reach that next level of play.

LET'S GO!

 ## POWER QUOTE

"Taking initiative is a form of self-empowerment."

—STEPHEN R. COVEY

 ## KEY INSIGHT

One of the most important principles for growth is simply leaning in to a new pursuit or goal and surrendering to the will and the power of the process to get there.

TACTICAL TIP

Take control of your day. You are where you need to be and you have the power to position yourself in learning situations. Find a way to open your mind to a new learning opportunity and take the initiative to lean into a new area of learning.

 ## DAY CHECK

What new goal or area of learning did you lean into today? How did you take the initiative to step out into a new aspect of life? What did you learn?

CHOOSE

I WANT TO SHARE with you a true story. It is my story, but it is not only my story. It is our story. It is your story. It is all of our stories in some way.

The power of story to resonate, connect and transform is un-rivaled. There is no better way to connect the human race to one another than through a powerful and resonant story to which people can relate.

It was the summer of 2012. I was in my first year of parole after being released from prison. I had served three and a half years for causing a boat accident.

I had adjusted to my new life outside with considerably more freedom than I had previously in that wretched place. There I had no freedom or identity. I was just a number to the state. I remember the day vividly—the sights and the smells, the feelings of that moment.

I was sitting in the mountains of the Adirondacks on a warm and sunny day in May. The air was a little humid, which was rare for the mountains. I felt like I was sweating, which was bizarre as it was only seventy-five degrees and I was sitting in the shade on the porch.

I sat in my grandfather's old rocking chair, nervously rocking back and forth. I had the last letter in my hand from the law and business schools to which I had applied.

I was so incredibly anxious to open the letter, worried that I would read the same result that I had read in the prior six letters:

"Rejected! Denied! We regret to inform you...." I could feel my heart beating faster, the air getting heavier, the rocking chair rocking faster.

I remembered the last time I had to open a letter with a fateful decision for my life. It was two years earlier when I was up for parole. I was denied and had to serve an additional two years.

I was devastated by that blow, essentially resentenced and told that despite my life transformation, all the hard work and model behavior, I would need to serve another two years.

I was completely defeated after that decision—but I never gave up.

My heart was racing faster and faster as I unfolded the letter and began to read, "We would like to thank you for your application to join Cornell University. Cornell University is a blah blah blah...."

Where is the decision! I exclaimed in impatience. I kept reading until I got to the middle of the second paragraph—and then my eyes met the cold reality.

"We regret to inform you that your application has been denied."

My dreams and vision for my future that I had worked so hard for over the previous two years finishing my undergraduate degree, studying and excelling on the LSAT admission test, rebuilding my life and turning it around—had been forever dashed and denied.

I was in complete shock and disbelief. My heart started to beat even harder and more noticeably, I started to genuinely worry about my future and what I was going to do.

I now had been rejected from seven graduate school programs for a combined law and business degree. *Seven!*

I had scored well on the LSAT graduate admission test. I had a strong resume and grades from undergraduate studies at Syracuse University. I had letters from community members about my life transformation and a passionate essay and theme to my application on my turnaround story of redemption.

But none of that mattered. I was denied the opportunity by people I have never met to pursue a new life and direction that I had dreamed of and worked tirelessly for. I didn't know what I was going to do. I was twenty-nine years old, reading my last rejection letter for the future that I thought was going to be mine, the one I had dreamed of since I was a child.

I had plans of going to Wall Street, climbing the corporate ladder and being a titan of industry in the financial world.

Denied. Rejected.

You cannot do that because we say you cannot do that.

I sat there wondering, worrying, trying to find words. I was twenty-nine years old with no job, no money or savings, no job prospects, no driver's license, no car, no belongings, no house or apartment of my own, on parole, with a curfew, attached at the hip to the state—with no future and no ability to find a path forward at that moment.

I had no idea what I was going to do, until...

I had one of the most impactful moments of clarity I've ever had in my entire life.

I realized right there on that porch that the only way I was going to achieve my vision for a massive life of achievement, contribution and impact, was to become an entrepreneur in every sense of the word.

I realized in that moment that I could not leave my future in the hands of others to choose if I was worthy enough.

I refused to give up. I will never give up.

I was not going to let some committee, hiring manager, head hunter, or anyone tell me I couldn't do something.

No. I refused to let that happen.

In that moment, I gained so much clarity, power and purpose, that it almost knocked me off that rocker—literally. I got up immediately and threw the letter in the trash.

I walked into the office and started to write a business plan for what would become, a few short years later, my first of three multimillion-dollar companies that I have founded and grown.

I began to chart and write out my vision for the future, for what I wanted my life to look like, for my goals, values and master plan to get there.

One door shut firmly in my face, but it opened up a far greater door to a new future. It was up to me to recognize that truth and react accordingly.

But I had a lot of work to do. The shift and transition were acute, painful and poignant in the moment; it would take weeks and months to make.

But I pivoted.

I found strength in denial and failure, clarity and a resolve to never give up. You see, every journey along the path to greatness and redemption starts in adversity and is decorated with conflict, setback and failure. No one who has ever achieved redemption, greatness, wealth, fame or significance and had a massive impact in the world, has done so with a smooth road. I was ready. I was focused. I chose to live a life of purpose, impact, contribution and achievement.

What will you choose to do?

LET'S GO!

POWER QUOTE

"Failure is simply the opportunity to begin again, this time more intelligently."

—HENRY FORD

KEY INSIGHT

Every journey to greatness and redemption starts in adversity and is decorated with conflict, setback and failure. No one who has ever achieved greatness, wealth, fame and significance has done so with a smooth road.

TACTICAL TIP

Think about adversity in your life situation. How might the setback in your life be a door closing so a bigger one will open? Are you letting other people define you when you should define success for yourself?

DAY CHECK

Think about the hard parts of today that made you feel like a failure. What did you learn from those hard parts? Think about how, because you struggled, you learned something new.

SHIFT YOUR MINDSET

WE'RE OFTEN FACED with critical choices in life that will have monumental and life-changing implications and consequences based on our decision.

We often don't see those consequences when we're in the moment, faced with a decision.

I had three life-altering and life-changing decisions to make with distinct forks in the road in my mid-20s. They would eventually shape who I became as an adult, how I live my life, where I am today and where I am going in the future.

I developed the following system to help break through the toughest of challenges and situations with an ironclad commitment, mindset shift and a will to persevere through any struggle:

STEP 1: COURAGE

This is the first critically important step in the process and transformation. It is where we need to get extremely honest and vulnerable with ourselves. We must let ego, pride and self-importance fall away in pursuit of truth and reality.

This is not always easy because the mind creates constructions and rationalizations to deal with challenges and difficult circumstances.

We often find ways to describe, minimize, or otherwise explain away really challenging times. We have a tendency as humans to use outside reasons, forces, or other things to explain why we face difficulty.

However, the only way we can develop this mindset shift and break through these walls to emerge on the right side of history is to take 100% responsibility and ownership over our behavior and circumstances.

Even if there are outside influences that ultimately contributed to wherever we are in life, whatever we are facing is a function of our decisions and behaviors and habits up to that point.

Don't ever forget that.

STEP 2: CONFRONT

The second step is to confront our current situation and circumstances head-on, make no excuses and take accountability. Accept the truth about the past and where you are in the present moment.

What is critical here is admitting that our past does not have to equal our future. There's so much power in this statement.

When we realize that in any one moment the rest of our lives can change and be radically different based on a shift in mindset and behavior, the world opens up for us.

It is critical that we accept the truth of our circumstances and confront head-on where we are and what we need to change.

STEP 3: VISION

The third step is vision. This comes down to getting crystal clear on what it is you're seeking in life.

What is truly important to you? What is going to drive you each and every day to commit to the vision and the plan that you set?

This is where you identify your *why* and what will guide and push you through the low points in the challenge.

This is where you need to get really honest and find what you are working toward, where you want to arrive and how you cross the gap between where you are today and where you want to be.

This is a creative process that can be both abstract and highly defined with plans, timelines and goals.

You need to define your vision and what the goal or destination looks like, so you can formulate a strategy and plan on how you're going to get there.

STEP 4: STRATEGY

This step focuses on laying out a plan with habits, behavior changes, actions and a timeline for how you're going to actually execute and move toward where you want to be. You'll want to identify three things:

- *Goals and priorities*
- *Steps and tactics*
- *The ONE thing that will be the critical success factor to not simply move the needle but to blast the needle off the gauge*

An example of this is when I knew that I simply could never, and should never, drink alcohol again. It was one of the key factors that led to one of the worst things in my life. It took me a while to fully grasp and accept that this was not simply an accident.

I had to develop a comprehensive system to support myself; otherwise, I was not going to be able to remain true and committed.

As part of your strategy, find and maintain motivation for your commitment. You'll want to know the past you want to change and the real emotional consequences to the behavior you're trying to change.

STEP 5: ACTION

This last capstone step is extremely important.

The system relies on completing each step fully before moving on to the next. It is absolutely essential and critical that after the four first four steps have been completed, we take massive and consistent action each and every day toward our vision.

To do that, we need to:

- *Develop a schedule and a timeline*
- *Develop an accountability system*
- *Win the morning and win the day by implementing success habits*

We need to focus on health, habits, morning and evening routines. We need to establish flow and create an environment that's conducive to transformation, progress and achievement.

We need to take massive action and steps. We must never be swayed by discouragement, but keep moving forward no matter what.

I encourage you to try this system to shift your mindset and achieve results when faced with any sized obstacle, wall, adversity, or setback.

It's going to take quite a bit of intentional effort to break free and emerge on the other side stronger and more purposeful, but...

You can do it!

LET'S GO!

 POWER QUOTE
_____

"The path to success is to take massive, determined action."

—TONY ROBBINS

 KEY INSIGHT
_____

You need to define your vision and what the goal or destination looks like so you can formulate a strategy and plan for how you're going to get there.

TACTICAL TIP

What is holding you back from making a change in your life? Is there really something holding you back, or are you choosing not to take the first step? Write down some things that you think are holding you back. Now write down solutions, even crazy solutions. Free all your creativity and problem-solving skills!

 DAY CHECK

What massive action did you start today? What obstacle did you push past?

NEVER LOSE FAITH

I **REMEMBER THE SCENE** vividly. I was traveling down the highway with my girlfriend during winter in upstate New York when she started to discuss her job.

She was considering a career shift because she didn't think she was making enough money for the time she spent there and what she was contributing.

I asked her what she was making at the time and what she thought she should be making. She replied that she was making about $70,000 but thought she should be making closer to $85,000 per year.

I remember the feeling in my gut when she told me that. It wasn't a feeling of consternation, anxiety, or jealousy. It was an extreme feeling of frustration and deep discouragement that swept over me.

You see, I was twelve months into my path of selling real estate, but I hadn't made one penny of income. I didn't have one sale. I had invested over $40,000 from a loan on advertising, marketing and start-up costs to get going in this business.

She asked why I was so quiet all of a sudden. I responded that I agree she should ask for a raise or consider a career path change because I agreed that her time and contributions were not being reflected in her salary.

But I couldn't get past the deep-seated emotions of self-doubt and discouragement I had felt. Why weren't things working out for me? Why wasn't I able to make even one sale?

I was told by veterans in the industry that it usually takes three to six months to get a sale and start up. Then it usually takes six to twelve months, or often longer, to start to really build a reliable real estate practice.

But I was already in month twelve! I had been so patient and diligent. I had worked so hard! Why had I not seen any return from the fruits of my labor?

I felt so discouraged and defeated in that car ride, and that feeling persisted for the next few days.

I remember thinking back to other times in my life when I had feelings of discouragement and defeat, where I started to lose hope in the possibility and prospect that I would be successful and be able to create a new life on a new path after what had happened.

I began to think of the mindset-shifting system that I had created at the other three major turning points in my life, where I had managed to generate the courage to move forward, despite extreme adversity and negative circumstances.

I found power and solace in that. I found the will to keep going, to work harder than anybody else and continue to put one foot in front of the other.

I determined to do what I needed to do with the faith that it would all work out soon *if I could just get over that little hump.*

Less than a month later, my very first property sold!

After that, another one sold, and another one. All of a sudden, the sum of my hard work and determination started to pay off.

I went from not making any money at all, and actually losing $40,000 my first year in the business, to becoming one of the top producers at my company in all of Upstate New York.

I then decided to form my own team to handle the exponential growth we were experiencing from the first two years as an individual agent.

By working hard, being patient, being resourceful and looking for other opportunities, I've been able to branch off, start and grow several seven-figure, real-estate-related businesses in hospitality development, commercial and residential property investment and more.

Why do I say all of this, and why does it matter to you?

I was inches from throwing in the towel out of discouragement, self-doubt and a lack of confident thinking that maybe this wasn't the right career path. *Maybe I should try something else.*

I thought about walking away because I hadn't made any money for a year. I thought about giving it all up to go pursue a traditional job and career path where I knew I would not be happy and fulfilled.

But I didn't.

I kept going, pushing through and finding a way to manufacture the courage and resolve I needed to break through that wall and enjoy success.

You see, most people give up when they're inches away from success. Most people walk away in the face of adversity and obstacles.

We're all naturally programmed to take the path of least resistance, much like water always runs downhill. However, that doesn't get us to a point of greatness and self-maximization.

We need to never lose faith in our ability to overcome challenges and setbacks, to rise above through the circumstances and the noise and to realize our vision and the success, purpose and impact that we were meant to have in this life.

Each and every one of us is destined for greatness. Each and every one of us is destined to have a massive impact in this world.

Each and every one of us deserves and should have all of the abundance, prosperity, respect and the fruits of our labors.

So get out there today and never give up on your dreams.

Never let setbacks or challenges frustrate you and your will to succeed. Never waver from the path you know you're meant to be on.

Always stay true to yourself, your vision and your values.

LET'S GO!

 ## POWER QUOTE

"Many of life's failures are people who did not realize how close they were to success when they gave up."

—THOMAS EDISON

 ## KEY INSIGHT

Never lose faith in your ability to overcome challenges, to rise above the chaos and to realize your purpose and impact you were meant to have in this life.

 ## TACTICAL TIP

Think about your goals in life. Do you have them written down? If not, write down your goals where you can see them every day. This will serve as a daily reminder to push through struggles because you deserve to reach your goals.

 ## DAY CHECK

What struggles did you push past today? What was your motivation to push past resistance?

IDENTITY

I WAS ONCE ASKED on a coaching call, "How do I change my beliefs around money?" The person's beliefs were that if they make more money, they will be greedy.

Therefore, when they make more money, they must give it away or spend it quickly. They even felt like they should avoid the actions required to get it in the first place.

It's very important to understand something: the strongest force in human personality is the need to remain consistent in how we define ourselves—our identity.

If you hold an identity (one of the strongest forms of beliefs) of yourself, you will do whatever it takes, consciously or sub-consciously, to make that identity a reality.

In order to change your identity, you must realign your values and in turn, create a new identity that meets all of your core needs—certainty, variety, significance, connection, growth and contribution.

This will take action. The more identities you have that give you fulfillment in life, the better. For example, if your sole identity is being a mother, what will you do when your kids grow up? Or if your sole identity is that you are financially successful, what will happen when you lose a business or go bankrupt? You'll experience the emotional rollercoaster of loss of identity.

I've lost my identity before—and it's not fun. So ask yourself, what identities do you tell yourself you have?

If you need help identifying your identities, I'll give you a clue. Look for anything that starts with "I am...."

And do they serve you well? If they don't serve you, think about the things you value the most. See how you can realign what it is you want to be doing to meet your values and needs.

LET'S GO!

 ## POWER QUOTE

"I am: Two of the most powerful words, for what you put after them shapes your reality."

—GARY HENSEL

 ## KEY INSIGHT

The strongest force in human personality is the need to remain consistent in how we define ourselves—our identity.

TACTICAL TIP

Write down your identities. If you have trouble finding them, write "I am..." then what you think you are. Which ones make you feel fulfilled and which don't?

 DAY CHECK

What are some words that would describe the identities you resonated with today? If someone met you and stayed with you all day, what words would they use after "(Your Name) is..."?

PART THREE

ENERGY

*Cultivating and sustaining a high level
of energy is critical to your success.*

ENERGY IS CRITICAL to your success and happiness. Energy is the spice of life. When you meet somebody who is energetic and enthusiastic about their life and their work, it's infectious. It's contagious. It brings you closer and invites connection and inspiration.

We always need to be mindful of our level of energy and develop habits, routines and frameworks to keep our energy high throughout the day in order to perform at our best and live an inspired life.

For me, I've always naturally had a high level of energy and intensity, probably due to my personality type being an ENTJ, high on the D on the DISC test, and a typical Type A personality that has an extreme commitment to whatever I put my mind to.

This has certainly served me well, but by no means is energy a trait you are either born with or without. Energy is something that we can develop; it is something that we can sustain; it is something that we can transfer to others to inspire and energize them, as well.

One of the frameworks and set of routines that I follow and embrace to help keep my energy level high throughout the day is a system of 11 daily habits. I track and measure these on a daily and weekly basis, and try to hit as close to 11 a day as I can.

Usually, I achieve 10 or 11. Some days if I'm traveling, I hit only 8 or 9. But when I'm hitting at least 9 or 10 out of 11, I know that I'm having a good day. I'll have a high level of energy in whatever activity or interaction I am having. Energy drives us. Energy sells.

Energy propels us forward toward our vision and our goals. Energy is the sustenance and fuel for living an Inspired Life. People want to be around, interact with and work with those who are energetic and enthusiastic about their life and their life's work. The following intentions will help you be more conscious, more mindful, and give you actionable strategies for increasing and sustaining a high level of energy.

GET THE FREE DOWNLOAD—*7 Frameworks to Live an Inspired Life—at LiveInspiredBook.com*

CONTROL YOUR HEALTH

I ENTERED A NEW year recently with a nasty viral illness. It took me out of commission. I was totally floored and bedridden just as I was ready, amped and fired-up to hit the ground running to begin the new year.

I learned a lot from this sickness and from the reasons why I got sick. I was vulnerable to external forces because my immune system was at a reduced state of operation. I hadn't gotten enough consistent good sleep and my diet had been neglected—as my doctor pointed out.

A few weeks later, I was at a meeting with a lady who told me she had advanced-stage cancer that had spread throughout her body.

She sat there and warned us about the dangers of eating processed food—and what it did to her and how she was facing a terminal illness.

She went into the details of how this happened—how her doctors had explained the carcinogens in the world, and the exposure she had to them. She warned us to watch what we eat and only eat a healthy, organic, plant-based diet to live a long life. This scared me. Hugely.

I had also watched a documentary on this very subject. The food industry in the United States is a multi-billion dollar industry, with entrenched interests from fertilizer and seed companies to drug and livestock treatments.

It is influenced by multinational companies that sell the end product to fast food companies, processed meat companies—you name it.

We're really facing an epidemic, and we are not even fully aware of it. I'm not bringing this up to scare or frighten you.

I'm sharing it because it shook me to my core and made me realize how important it is in life to control the things I can—my diet, my fitness, my mindset and my surroundings. After all, there is so much we cannot control in the world.

So, I went on a cleanse and a vegan challenge for a month. I then modified it a bit and have been following a strict pescatarian diet since, and have never felt and been healthier. I want to encourage and suggest that you give it a try yourself.

It won't be easy, but it will be liberating.

If I want to continue producing at the level I am now for all of my life, I know I need to be healthy and live a long life to make my massive vision a reality.

It's important to find and maintain peak health throughout our lives in order to live our dreams and provide what we want for our families and those around us.

Getting sick as I turned the corner that year took a lot out of me. It opened my eyes and made me realize that I cannot get anything done and be my productive self if I am not healthy first.

It was hugely frustrating, as I had a lot of work and goals I wanted to work on in the new year—but I couldn't.

My doctor said not getting the proper sleep and being stressed was likely the reason my immune system was down. I had gotten sick three times in the last three months. I had lost almost three weeks!!

Crazy!

I want to encourage you to make nutrition, fitness, sleep, meditation and life balance a huge priority. If you don't address these areas of life and make them your top priorities, the rest means nothing.

Make your health a major priority for you today!

LET'S GO!

 ## POWER QUOTE

"Investing in our health is the biggest investment we will ever make."

—ELLIE SAVOY

KEY INSIGHT

It's important to find and maintain peak health throughout our lives in order to live our dreams and provide what we want for our families and those around us.

 ## TACTICAL TIP

Think about your daily health habits. Do you sleep enough? Do you eat more non-processed food than processed? Do you drink the required water amount? Do you exercise daily? These are all important things that keep you healthy and fit to reach your goals. What healthy habits are you going to create to kickstart your health?

 ## DAY CHECK

What habits did you notice today that are unhealthy and healthy? What will you do differently tomorrow?

POSITIVE ENERGY

A KEY INGREDIENT, AND in my mind the leading factor in creating a successful and positive culture for your team or organization, is positive energy.

Here are a few powerful excerpts from *The Energy Bus* by Jon Gordon, a book I highly recommend:

> *Positive energy. . . . It's a term being talked about a lot more frequently in conference rooms, classrooms, locker rooms, and even living rooms. Perhaps it's because there is an abundance of new research that shows that positive people, positive communication, positive interactions, and positive work and team cultures produce positive results. Or perhaps at a deeper level we all know that every person, every career, every company, every organization, every family, and every team will have to overcome negativity, adversity, and challenges to define themselves and to chart the course into the future they want, desire and deserve.*
>
> *No one goes through life untested, and the answer to these tests is positive energy—not the rah-rah, cheering kind of positive energy, although there certainly is a time and a place for that, as well.*

*But rather, when I talk about positive energy I'm referring
to the optimism, trust, enthusiasm, love, purpose, joy, passion, and spirit to live, work, and perform at a higher level;
to build and lead successful teams; to overcome adversity
in life and at work; to share contagious energy with employees, colleagues, and customers; to bring out the best
in others and in yourself; and to overcome all the negative
people (whom I call energy vampires) and negative situations that threaten to sabotage your health, family, team,
and success.[7]*

This passage stuck with me. It hit me on a number of different
levels.

I've had my share of struggles when I was younger, and I have
had some really, really low bottoms. I had to hit and experience
the lows in order to reach moments of clarity and honesty.

Sometimes you need to get really vulnerable and honest in
order to really grow.

When I was at my lowest, I had a choice. Let the emotions
and situation consume me and the rest of my life, or choose
the alternative—marshall all of my faculties and resources, and
manufacture all of that into a burning desire and positive energy to propel me into a life of deliberate purpose, intentional
living and massive contribution to the world.

The power of positive energy in my life has been so overwhelming that it's hard to describe.

---

[7]   Jon Gordon, "Introduction" in *The Energy Bus* (Wiley, 2007).

I am such a firm believer, based on my life experience, in the strength and power of positive thought, envisioning outcome and energetic living.

I attract the things I want into my life. Do you know how this is done?

It's done through embracing an unwavering commitment to always looking at life and its myriad of situations, setbacks and challenges as opportunities for growth, not reasons for despair, negativity or excuses.

When you do this, life opens up.

What does this approach to a positive attitude and life do for our cultures?

Well, it's arguably one of, if not the most, important and fundamental ingredients in the recipe for creating really great cultures.

Positive energy, enthusiasm and a *joie de vivre* are contagious—they attract other people to them.

Colleagues, potential clients, partners, friends—you name it—people want to be around people who are full of positive energy, who exude confidence and peace of mind, who are strong and stoic and unwavering in their demeanor and attitude in the face of adversity and setbacks.

These are the traits of a true leader.

These are the things that make for a really strong culture that attracts the RIGHT people into its orbit, those that share and can relate to the values embraced and want to be a part of the story.

LET'S GO!

 ## POWER QUOTE

"If you are positive, you'll see opportunities instead of obstacles."

—WIDAD AKRAWI

 ## KEY INSIGHT

Positive energy, enthusiasm and a joie de vivre are contagious—they attract other people to them.

 ## TACTICAL TIP

What energy will you put out today? Do people see you as a positive person or a negative person? How do you see yourself? Make a point to be positive and see how it affects your day and those around you.

 ## DAY CHECK

How did your positivity affect your day? If you got negative, how did that affect your day?

UNSHAKEABLE

THE FOLLOWING PASSAGE from *Unshakeable* by Tony Robbins provides a great definition of the word:

An unwavering and undisputed confidence; a steadfast commitment to the truth; presence, peace of mind, and a calm amidst the storm.

What would it feel like to know in your mind, in your heart and in the very depth of your soul that you'll always be prosperous?

To know with absolute certainty that no matter what happens in the economy, stock market, or real estate, you'll have financial security for the rest of your life?

To know that you'll possess an abundance that will enable you to not only take care of your family's needs but also to delight in the joy of helping others?

We all dream of achieving that tremendous inner peace, that comfort, that independence, that freedom. In short, we all dream of being unshakeable.

I really liked this opening to his book. It resonated with me on a number of levels.

Through my own obstacles and challenges, I was able to build on a strong will and constitution I had developed early on in my life.

I created a backbone of confidence and strength, rooted in a strong sense of self and personal values and principles on which I placed priority.

When we are able to have full confidence in ourselves, abilities, what we stand for and can still remain teachable amidst this confidence, self assuredness and awareness, we are truly approaching a beautiful state that is rooted in a stoic commitment to our beliefs and principles.

You may ask, *"Why does all of this matter?"*

It matters because now, more than ever, we are inundated on a daily basis with information, negativity, changing attitudes, trends and unforeseen events and catastrophes.

I want to ask you to take ten minutes at some point during the day today.

Only ten minutes.

Find a quiet place, take a pen and paper, think about the following questions and then write down your answers.

After you write your answers to these questions, I want to ask you to internalize what you wrote. Repeat what you wrote out loud, affirm it and put it out into the world. Then go about your normal morning routine and day.

- *What are your five most important values or principles that you live your life by and that you seek out in those you choose to have in your life?*

- *What are your five biggest motivators, the things that contribute to your WHY and the reasons why you work so hard and have the goals you have?*

Then I want to ask that you take another five to ten minutes at the end of your day, during your nightly routine, and do a simple review of your day—a mini-audit if you will.

Think about all that happened, all of the issues and challenges of the day, the triumphs and the successes.

- *Were your behaviors and actions true to your values?*

- *When the world around you fell out of balance, did you fall with it—or did you stay true to your core?*

- *Were you stoic and unshakeable in moments of distress and uncertainty, or were you calm and at peace with your course of action?*

- *Were your actions and accomplishments driven by the motivators you wrote down, or were they driven by the needs of others, external events, or things you hadn't planned?*

I think you will find this to be a helpful exercise. I know I did.

It shouldn't take more than fifteen minutes total in your day, and can often be quite illuminating toward helping you become *unshakeable.*

LET'S GO!

POWER QUOTE

"Freedom doesn't mean the absence of all restrictions, it means possessing unshakable conviction in the face of any obstacle."

—DAISAKU IKEDA

KEY INSIGHT

When we are able to have full confidence in ourselves, abilities, what we stand for and can still remain teachable amidst this confidence, self assuredness and awareness, we are truly approaching a beautiful state that is rooted in a stoic commitment to our beliefs and principles.

TACTICAL TIP

Write down your five most important values or principles that you live your life by. Then list your five biggest motivators.

DAY CHECK

Were your behaviors and actions true to your values? When the world around you fell out of balance, did you fall with it—or did you stay true to your core?

PRESS ON

ONE OF THE most important things is life is perseverance—giving 120% commitment and effort to overcom-
ing everything and every challenge or obstacle in life.

One of the keys to perseverance is knowing how to detach
emotion and expectation from the ultimate outcome and trust
in the process.

It's critical to know that, no matter the ultimate result, you did
everything you possibly could to achieve what you sought to
achieve and left everything out on the field.

The passion that we bring to the table in every endeavor we
undertake in life will drive the outcome and the success of our
efforts.

However, even if we are the most passionate we could possibly be, even if what we are fighting for is so blatantly apparent and right and value-driven, even if all the evidence in
the world supports our case and what we are fighting for—we
could still experience a negative outcome.

That's because there are some decisions and things out of our
control. Others still have the power to dictate and wield influence and power over determining the outcome.

What we need to realize is that we cannot control or influence every outcome that may impact us.

It's not possible.

We need to be laser focused on our mission, values and strategy in order to continue to be successful. We need to trust in the process and detach expectation and emotion from the outcome and focus on the effort, on what needs to be done.

If there is a negative outcome, at least you know you gave everything you possibly had.

The trials I have gone through have made me stronger, more resolute, focused and mindful of my mission statement and core values.

I am more persistent now than ever before; I persevere and I trust that no matter the outcome, I don't regret anything in the effort and in the process.

I give it all that I can and let the universe decide the rest.

LET'S GO!

 POWER QUOTE

"Nothing in the world can take the place of persistence. Talent will not; nothing is more common than unsuccessful men with talent. Genius will not; unrewarded genius is almost a proverb. Education will not; the world is full of educated derelicts. Persistence and determination alone are omnipotent. The slogan, 'press on' has solved, and always will solve, the problems of the human race."

—CALVIN COOLIDGE

 ## KEY INSIGHT

We need to be laser focused on our mission, values and strategy in order to continue to be successful. We need to trust in the process and detach expectation and emotion from the outcome and focus on the effort, on what needs to be done.

 ## TACTICAL TIP

When talking to coworkers or anyone else during the day about something you want, try detaching your emotion from the outcome of the discussion and your determination to press on.

 ## DAY CHECK

How did you detach your emotions from an outcome today so you could keep moving forward regardless of the outcome? In what situations did you not? How did these two feelings differ?

NEGATIVE NEWS

OFTEN TIMES WHEN we're confronted with bad or negative news or any external circumstance, our initial reaction can be one that is not always healthy or positive.

For me, one of my strongest qualities is an extreme and passionate commitment to whatever I put my mind to, but the polar opposite of this is also true, and can be my kryptonite—which is an extreme commitment to the same level of passion in a response to a negative event or emotion.

I don't always step away, compartmentalize and move on as quickly as I would like to.

I've been working on this. There's a lot of benefit to being more *aware* of our reactions and thoughts rather than actually *in* them.

Mindfulness exercises work well, developing a stoic attitude when you can keep an even-keeled equilibrium despite negative or external circumstances or events that might ordinarily cause you to lose focus and attention on what is at hand.

I know we all experience this, things that may happen in our business or life that are unexpected and catch us completely off guard. These things can put us in a bind or an uncomfortable position.

However, we always have a choice as to how we will react and deal with that situation.

The strategy and tactics I'm embracing to try to improve how I deal with events like this are born from a traditional theory in psychology known as cognitive behavioral therapy.

It's based upon the idea that a thought that comes into our head invokes a feeling or emotion, which produces a behavior. It is the realization that for any negative, unpleasant, or regrettable behavior, we have to trace back to the emotion which elicited and prompted that behavior. From there, we must ask, "what was the initial thought that created that feeling or emotion?"

We have an ability to train ourselves through breathing, meditation, trigger words and other mindfulness hacks to pull ourselves out of the immediate reaction that we have following a negative event.

We need to remove and look at our thoughts as if we're outside of our body from afar looking in.

The theory goes that we can replace the negative thoughts that come into our minds, which then trigger the emotions and feelings of frustration, which then lead to the behavior of overreacting or losing focus.

So, if we can catch ourselves and replace that initial negative thought with a more positive thought, it will have a ripple effect down the line from the emotion and the behavior that manifests.

I can begin to get outside of my body and my framework, and even if I don't agree with another point of view, I can at least appreciate it.

I can see what they believe and what they think is true based on the lens that they're looking through from their life experiences and unique circumstances.

By doing this, we can realize that our thoughts do not have to become our actions and our entire world. We have options about how we respond to negative news.

We can let thoughts come into our minds and just as easily leave our minds, and we can train with discipline, if we choose to.

By doing that we can start to create a more balanced, a more reasoned, a calmer and more productive response to those negative external events that will always come into our lives.

When we do this, we can have better reactions, relationships, and interactions and not lose focus on what we need to be concentrating on just because something came up that was unfortunate and unforeseen.

LET'S GO!

 POWER QUOTE

"Change your thinking, change your life."

—ERNEST HOLMES

KEY INSIGHT

We always have a choice as to how we will react and deal with negative news.

 ## TACTICAL TIP

Think of an instance in which you were being criticized by another person. How did you feel? Now think about how the other person felt. If you were that person, how would you feel? Put yourself in another's shoes.

 ## DAY CHECK

How did you calm yourself down from a stressful situation today? Did you stop and think, or react in the moment?

PART FOUR

SUCCESS

Your level of success in any area of your life is a function of the magnitude of your vision, your mindset and your actions.

S UCCESS IS DIFFERENT for everyone. Success for
some people is professional and monetary achievement.
Success for others is deep, meaningful relationships. For some
people, success is raising a family and contributing to them
and the community. Success holds some common denomina-
tors no matter how you define it and leaves clues as to what it
takes to be successful in any area of life.

Success for me is knowing I've given everything I can to whatever I choose to commit my time and energy to. Success for
me is knowing that I am showing up and living in my true purpose, constantly growing and working toward achieving my
true potential in every area of life.

Success for me is not having any regrets and not wishing I
had done things differently or better. Success for me is seeing
the results of my hard work and the impact and contribution
they make to improving the lives of others and this world as
a whole.

Success is more simplistic than we often make it seem. Our
level of success is dictated by the magnitude of our vision for
life, the expansiveness of our mindset, the capacity to think,
dream and plan to make this grand vision a reality. It's determined by the size of the massive action it will take in a consistent manner to make this mission an actual reality.

What is success for you? How do you define success, and how are you working diligently toward achieving success in your life?

The following intentions and strategies will help you become more successful in all areas of your life if you implement them and commit to them in a consistent manner.

GET THE FREE DOWNLOAD—*7 Frameworks to Live an Inspired Life*—at *LiveInspiredBook.com*

GET VULNERABLE

IT'S IMPORTANT TO be vulnerable at times. In fact, in certain situations it can be powerful.

The definition of vulnerability is this:

Capable of being physically or emotionally wounded. It can also mean susceptible to judgment or negative outcomes.

Vulnerability is a difficult concept for many people. By being vulnerable, we open ourselves up to emotional trauma, unrealized expectations, judgment and rejection.

Being honest and transparent with sharing thoughts, experiences, or ideas with others requires courage and honesty—and there is a risk.

You can only make meaningful connections by opening yourself up, being vulnerable and exposing things about yourself to others. This is what creates trust and deep connections.

I have found, through my experiences, five key ways in which vulnerability can increase your happiness and success:

1. CREATE MEANINGFUL RELATIONSHIPS

With relationships, there's no substitute for self-expression. Expressing yourself lets people know who you are and your character traits.

The higher vulnerability you show, the greater risk you take, but also the greater chance you have to connect with someone.

2. BE OPEN TO CONSTRUCTIVE CRITICISM

Learning how to take constructive criticism is a huge talent and skill. It takes practice and courage. I'm not great at it, to be honest. I want to be accepted, liked and know I have performed my best.

Vulnerability allows you the opportunity to grow in a way that constantly being closed off does not. Realizing we may not be right nor have the best idea is a learning moment for growth— if we are open to it.

3. SHARE NEW IDEAS AND THOUGHTS

When you open yourself up, not everyone will agree nor appreciate it. You risk judgment, rejection and emotional pain.

But this is where breakthroughs and connections happen.

4. BE CREATIVE

Putting yourself, your work and your art out there takes courage. But what results can come of it? Exposure, acclaim and success.

Are you ready to take the risk to achieve the reward and the greatness that can come from true creativity and to share this with the world?

5. SHOW STRENGTH

Being able to reveal both positive and negative parts about yourself is a demonstration of strength.

The more vulnerable you make yourself, the greater the risk you're taking, but greater are the rewards that can be reaped.

On the other hand, if you don't reveal much, but remain invulnerable, you're not going to get a lot in the way of rewards.

All of growth lies on the other side of fear.

In order to face our fears, we must be vulnerable.

I have found this through my experiences in life and have chosen to embrace the power of vulnerability.

What will you do today to embrace your own powerful vulnerability?

LET'S GO!

POWER QUOTE

"To share your weaknesses is to make yourself vulnerable; to make yourself vulnerable is to show your strength."

—CRISS JAMI

KEY INSIGHT

Vulnerability is a powerful concept and practice. It can help you move from areas of comfort and quietude to areas of discomfort, discovery and growth.

TACTICAL TIP

The first step of being vulnerable with others is being vulnerable with yourself. Are there places where you may be holding back from being candid with yourself about you?

DAY CHECK

Did you make a deeper connection with someone today by being vulnerable and open? How did it feel?

INTENTION 27

BALANCE

I **WANT TO TALK** about the importance of *living* life and not just *working* life.

It's about finding balance and making time to embrace the many pleasures we are fortunate to have in this life.

Many of us sometimes forget to make *living life* a priority, to block time and make it a regular part of life.

I presume you are a highly-ambitious, deliberate, purposeful and committed person. You probably work harder and smarter than most other people.

People like us build elaborate business plans and strategies. We implement big thinking and ideas. We attract, train and develop the best talent in our marketplace.

We often work really long hours and crush our goals and competition.

This is all awesome. This is what we love to do.

I absolutely love being an entrepreneur, creating the life of my dreams and doing it all by intention and design.

But what are we all working so hard *for*?

What is our big *why*, and how much are we actually enjoying the life we work so hard to create?

What are you doing for *you* today?

How much time are you taking to pursue your hobbies and your down time?

The answer for many of us might be *not enough*. I know I have often allowed my ambition and the growth of my businesses to be the number-one priority in my life for several years.

When I make those things a priority, a lot of my hobbies suffer. I don't spend the same amount of time on *me*, personal time to simply relax and enjoy all that I'm so fortunate to have.

Most of us have many things to be thankful for: our health, families, friends, teams, financial independence, the ability to create things—the list goes on and on.

But I know I haven't always taken the time to focus on *me* and simply *live* and enjoy life.

You need to be committed to shutting off and focusing on *you*, to finding that elusive work-life balance, staying grateful, humble, and spending time doing the things that you love to do.

Be committed not to working less, but rather to being more efficient with your time and embracing leverage more and more.

Commit to always doing what you love, always improving your craft and life—growing as an individual.

Commit to embracing and living life to the fullest each and every day and on your terms.

What will you commit to today?

LET'S GO!

 POWER QUOTE

"Carve out and claim the time to care for yourself and kindle your own fire."

—AMY IPPOLITI

 KEY INSIGHT

You need to be committed to shutting off and focusing on you, to finding that elusive work life balance, staying grateful, humble and spending time doing the things that you love to do.

 TACTICAL TIP

What are some things you enjoy? Take time out of your day today to do something you love to do.

DAY CHECK

How did you take time for yourself today?

YOUR EVENING ROUTINE

LET'S TALK ABOUT something that we easily overlook—
our evening routine.

Often we don't give the same amount of focus to maintaining a strong evening routine as we do our morning routine. But when you don't have a strong evening routine, it affects your next day and how you begin your morning routine.

I thought I would share with you what I do each evening to set myself up for success the next day. Now, to be candid, I don't always stick to all of it, but I try to hit many of the things on the list consistently.

For me, the biggest challenge in hitting a consistently strong evening routine is that I don't always turn off or end the work day when I should.

At the time of this writing, I'm single with no kids. I run four different businesses, so the demands on my time are great. I often stay and work at the office until nine or ten, sometimes even eleven or twelve at night.

More recently, I've been trying to turn off by seven-thirty or eight at the latest, review the day and plan the next, to work on what I call "a day's plan".

I plan out my weekly priorities for each of my businesses. I choose two or three things I must get done, as well as manage my time blocks, which is writing down major priorities for the next day.

I spend 10 or 15 minutes on this.

Then I usually go out to dinner with a friend, colleague or by myself. More and more, I am trying to eat a healthy dinner at home.

Now, I'm not a great cook, nor do I have the patience or the interest in cooking prep and clean up, so I hired a part-time Personal Assistant / Cook / Housekeeper. It's a great way for me to leverage someone else's expertise to simplify, automate and manage a lot of the domestic and household things that I'm not good at and don't really have time for.

As a result, I'm not eating out for every meal. Not only am I saving money, but I'm also managing what's going into my body better by eating salads, protein smoothies and healthy wraps during the week.

I know that if these healthy lifestyle management habits are taken care of, I can focus on what I'm best at—managing and growing my businesses.

The next thing I like to do in my evening routine is have a block for personal reading and project time, which is usually from eight until nine or nine-thirty. I'll read a book, maybe make a journal entry, or work on something of a personal nature.

Next, I'll do a quick two to three minute habit and routine review for the day. I have a spreadsheet that I use for my eleven things that I like to accomplish each day.

I make sure to put a check mark next to the ones I've done. Then I add up the checkmarks for a daily score; trying to hit at least nine out of eleven for each day signifies a good day.

Some of the actions on that daily habit tracker are exercise, meditate, read the news or my book for forty-five minutes to an hour, take my vitamins, drink five glasses of water, avoid negativity, follow my schedule for the day, achieve my goals for the day and engage my evening routine.

Then I might make a couple of personal phone calls to family or friends if I have any to call back. I try to be in bed by eleven. Unfortunately, sometimes I'll get to bed closer to midnight, and that's really not enough sleep for me.

I try to optimize by tracking and measuring my sleep. That's a huge area of health and personal management that is often overlooked—quality and length of sleep time.

Everybody needs a certain amount of sleep for the body and mind to rest and feel rejuvenated and recharged for the new day. Some people only need five hours of sleep, while other people need eight or even ten hours of sleep to be at their best.

One way to help sleep is to do a meditation at the end of the day or engage in a mindfulness practice.

I also try to do no coffee or caffeine after 4 p.m. I used to have coffee late, like an espresso after dinner. But that just kept my mind racing and didn't allow me to get into a deep sleep.

I track my sleep with two different technologies. One is called the Oura ring. It's a waterproof, fashionable ring with sensors that tracks all of your physiological body signs like body temperature, heart rate, the number of times that you wake up and roll over, your breathing, how long you sleep and how deep you sleep.

It's all tracked in the cloud with a nice app. It sends a report via email to you in the morning so you can see how you slept the prior night.

I also have a great memory foam mattress that's supportive and Alexa-enabled to heat and cool. I'm not going to lie, it's pretty sweet! It was a larger investment, but when you can talk to your mattress and tell it to warm up before you get in bed—and then it tracks your entire sleep pattern and sends you a report on how to maximize and improve—that's next generation!

So that's my evening routine. Again, I don't always hit it perfectly a hundred percent of the time, but if I'm hitting it at eighty percent, I know I'm doing pretty well.

I get ahead of the game by ending the day strong, so I can have an even stronger next day.

What's your evening routine?

LET'S GO!

 ## POWER QUOTE

"The secret of your future is hidden in your daily routine."

—MIKE MURDOCK

 ## KEY INSIGHT

Often we don't give the same amount of focus to maintaining a strong evening routine as we do our morning routine. But when you don't have a strong evening routine, it affects your next day and how you begin your morning routine.

 ## TACTICAL TIP

Take a minute to write a list of things you would like to do in your evening routine. Keep it simple and start implementing it this evening.

 ## DAY CHECK

How did your new evening routine go? Did you accomplish at least half of what you wanted to get done today? What do you need to adjust for tomorrow evening?

CREATE NEW EXPERIENCES

THERE'S SOMETHING I think is important for all of us to do regularly—create new experiences for ourselves and others in our lives.

Often we get focused on building our businesses, advancing our careers, households or just the day-to-day routines in life, and that's fine and noble. But we are not robots, we are human.

We are creative and need to breathe, journey and explore. Spontaneity, new experiences and travels make lasting memories, create new growth opportunities for personal enrichment, and create an awareness perspective and a new appreciation for all that we have to be grateful for.

One thing I've committed to doing is to take four pre-planned vacations each year at the end of each quarter. I have various business travels, some one or two-night getaway trips, a long weekend here and there, etc.

However, I'm trying to actually take time for these pre-planned vacations, and two of the vacations will be to places I've never been before.

You see, I realized I tend to rely on my usual trends and habits even in my travels. I tend to go to places that are comfortable and familiar, such as warm places in the Caribbean or Florida, although my regular travels often take me to Europe.

We are creatures of habit. We like what we like. If we really want to adventure and explore the world, to create new and enriching experiences, to experience different cuisines, histories, cultures and people, then we need to get out of our comfort zone.

We need to go to places we don't usually go.

Seeing how the rest of the world lives is really eye-opening. Most of the world doesn't have access to a fraction of what is available to people in the United States, where I live.

It's a great reminder for those that live in the U.S. to never take anything for granted and to be grateful for their freedom and opportunity.

When we are able to see and experience other places, even if for a short amount of time, it makes us more mindful and aware of what we have. It allows us to be more grateful and appreciative of all that we are fortunate to enjoy in our lives.

It helps us be more benevolent, charitable and generous. It allows us to grow, enrich and enlarge our lives and perspectives.

Get out of your comfort zone, not just by going to a beach or luxury resort, but rather by immersing yourself in a new culture and experience. It will feel uncomfortable at first.

Find comfort in the unfamiliarity. That's truly exploring and adventuring.

I encourage you to think about this when you book your next vacation or think about your next day trip or long weekend.

First, plan these things into your calendar. Second, instead of going to the same place or familiar place that you always like to go to, why not try someplace else?

If you haven't been out of the country, get a passport and research countries you've always been interested in, and start building an itinerary to some faraway land to truly explore something new and different.

Watch what this does to your mind and your soul. It's a truly amazing effect!

I guarantee you will want to continue to embrace new experiences as part of your life journey.

LET'S GO!

 POWER QUOTE
_____

"Life begins at the end of your comfort zone."

—NEALE DONALD WALSCH

KEY INSIGHT

Do something new and different. Get outside of your comfort zone. Plan an adventure and explore the world. Find a way to make an impact and make a difference today and everyday.

TACTICAL TIP

When is your next vacation opportunity? If you could go anywhere, where would you go? Try brainstorming ideas for new experiences that will stretch your comfort zone. Try new foods or visit new places around your work and home as a start today.

DAY CHECK

What new experience did you engage in today? How did it feel? Did you adjust and find comfort in being out of your comfort zone?

CLARITY

THE INDISPENSABLE FIRST step to getting the things you want out of life is to: *Decide what you want first.*

Earlier I shared my thoughts about finding your purpose, your *why*.

It's really important to know exactly what it is that you want— and what it is that drives you to want this—to actually be successful, fulfilled in your life and the pursuit and achievement of your dreams.

Clarifying your vision of an ideal life is important, in fact it is mission critical. Your vision should ideally include the following seven areas:

- *Work and career*
- *Finances*
- *Recreation and free time*
- *Health and fitness*
- *Relationships*
- *Personal goals*
- *Contribution and legacy*

It is not necessary to know exactly *how* you are going to get to your intended destination—all that is important is that you figure out where *there* is. If you get clear on the *what*, the *how* will show up in due time with perseverance.

High achievers like you have really massive visions for their lives. They define and lay out their vision; they tweak and revisit it; they keep it front and center.

The greater danger for most people is not the inability to achieve their goals in life, but that because their vision and goals are so small, they won't reach their true potential.

Think about that for a minute. That's powerful. Most people won't reach their potential in life due to not pushing themselves. They settle and fail to realize their true capabilities.

This is the tragedy. Don't settle for a vision that sells yourself short. Dream big and let that clarity drive you forward today.

LET'S GO!

 POWER QUOTE

"Whatever the mind can conceive and believe, it can achieve."

—NAPOLEON HILL

KEY INSIGHT

The greater danger for most people is not the inability to achieve their goals in life, but is rather because their vision and goals are so small that they won't reach their true potential.

 ## TACTICAL TIP

Do you sell yourself short when it comes to your work? Do you make small goals to play it safe? Although those goals have a place, you cannot sell yourself short of your true potential. Push yourself in your daily goals.

 ## DAY CHECK

What three things did you do today to move you toward achieving your purpose?

Please visit LiveInspiredBook.com for an exercise that can help you gain clarity in your life.

Here are a few questions to help you get started on this exercise:

- *How do you envision yourself as a leader in the future? Be as specific as possible.*

- *What personal qualities do you have right now that will help you achieve that vision? What ones do you want to grow? What ones do you want to change?*

- *What habits do you have in place currently, and what other habits do you see yourself developing to accomplish that vision?*

- *What are your goals regarding family, career, health, community and for you personally?*

- *Take a few minutes and picture how you see your life in the future. In a few detailed paragraphs, share your vision for where you see yourself in 10 years.*

- *What are you passionate about? What values guide your life? Make a detailed list of values you are committed to living by.*

YOUR CONTRIBUTION

H OW DO WE go from growth to contribution on the continuum of our personal and professional development in life?

One of the things we have to do is something that you probably value and spend a lot of time on—the idea of growth. If you're like me, you invest a lot of energy, time, effort and money into making sure you're always growing, learning, developing and advancing.

It's critical that each day and each experience is somehow incrementally better than what came before.

If we're not growing, we're dying—there is no middle.

There's not a lot that is static or that stays at stasis for long in this world. Look at any plants or living organisms or anything out there in the universe. It's either headed in the direction of up and growth, or down and decay.

I started to think about this a lot recently as I've been spending the last five or six years rebuilding my life. This has taken an insane amount of focus, dedication and hard work to get to where I am today.

I've done that by being diligent in building the skills and knowledge that are required to be successful in my career and in my personal life—on the terms that I define as success.

I'm grateful to have gotten to this position now where I've made this a way of life, but I'll always remain teachable and humble and eager to grow.

I'm not saying that I have arrived at my destination in any sense, because I think the destination is never truly achieved in life. We are always moving the goalposts and creating a new level or floor of success and growth from which we can build.

We need to cherish, be grateful and embrace the process, not simply the goal or destination where we want to ultimately be.

I think we all get to a point where I am starting to arrive now, where we realize that it's not just about growing ourselves. It's not just about the selfish focus on being the best that we can be. At some point we must shift to *contribution* if we are to reach the next level in our evolution as individuals.

You might ask what exactly do I mean by *contribution*?

Contribution is about helping others grow, learn and become better by teaching, leading and sharing the experience and the philosophy that we've gained through all of our efforts and growth.

Contribution is about putting yourself out there and helping others achieve something greater for themselves and their families.

Contribution can come from helping a childhood friend over-come a really difficult time in life through a relationship, job firing or any other obstacle or adversity that they might en-counter.

Contribution can come from volunteering in helping build your community, neighborhood or society by sharing your talent, skills and strengths with others.

For me, I am transitioning to starting a new chapter in life based on not just growth, as that should never end, but now, more importantly, on contribution.

Paying it forward. Putting out into the world and focusing more on serving and in the building of others, not just myself and my family.

So are you ready to move from growth to contribution in your professional and personal life?

How can you do more to serve, contribute and help others today?

Start small. It's the small acts over time that build to really meaningful results and impacts.

Today, find a new way to contribute and help others through sharing experiences, insights, knowledge and enthusiasm.

Do it with *no* expectation of getting anything in return—and see what happens.

LET'S GO!

 POWER QUOTE

"Help others achieve their dreams and you will achieve yours."

—LES BROWN

 KEY INSIGHT

Contribution is about putting yourself out there and helping others achieve something greater for themselves and their families.

 TACTICAL TIP

How can you serve people around you today? What do you have that can be used to lift others up? Think about ways to help others and pay attention to the feeling afterwards.

 DAY CHECK

How did you lift someone up today, without thinking of what you got out of it? How did it feel?

SYSTEMATIC ELEVATION

I T'S TIME TO think about a system I have developed that I call *Systematic Elevation*. By that, I mean a system and philosophy on life and achievement that I have developed and implemented to great benefit that I want to share.

Systematic Elevation is the careful, deliberate and methodical progression in any endeavor. It's the approach, the outlook and the strategy used to ascend and elevate from where you are to where you want to be.

It's a fact—to advance and grow, we must do things differently than we did before.

The world around us is ever-changing. We, too, must be ever-changing in the skills we identify and develop, the strategies and tactics we implement and follow and the mindset and worldview we adopt and maintain.

It's really the only way we're going to progress and grow in character, achievement and life expansion in every area and sense. The system of *Systematic Elevation* I follow looks like this:

- *I start my year (and revisit quarterly) reviewing and adapting my one-, three-, five- and ten-year plans.*

- *I then set really big mid- to long-term goals that both scare and excite me.*

- *Next, I develop a set strategy and sub-tactics I will implement to make sure these goals get achieved.*

- *I will then identify the resources, capital and people required to make the goal a reality.*

- *I then future-pace the development and growth required—in mind, body, faculties and resources—to achieve those large goals.*

- *After that I develop a tracking or monitoring mechanism, ideally with some form of lateral or mentor accountability system in place.*

- *Then comes what I view as probably the most important part of the system or philosophy—I view every success on each of these goals not as an achievement, or a destination, where a goal is accomplished—but rather as simply a new floor. It's a new, higher floor from which I can continue to build my vision for a massive life and business empire.*

This last part is critical. Fundamental, actually. Think of it this way: it's like you are building a house, brick by brick, layer by layer, until you establish a new floor.

What do you do on that new floor? You shouldn't merely pull out a rocker and sit back and rest. No, for me, this success simply motivates me to now work on building the house even higher, by working toward adding the next, higher floor to the home—a floor where I can then see farther across the world, the landscape, the horizon of opportunity.

The higher the floor, the farther you can see and the more wisdom you will gain—the better your ability to weather storms, to see paths through obstacles and to plan for future growth.

That's why this is the most important part of Systematic Elevation: remembering and embracing the notion that no goal is a destination, but rather a milestone on the road, or a higher floor in the house you are building for your life.

We need to always work to build higher floors or vantage points from which we can view and anticipate the changing world around us. These become places from which we can dream and grow, and enhance and enlarge our vision for our life and those around us.

So today, I encourage you to take some time and make a plan if you don't already have one. This is a comprehensive and involved plan for all areas of your life.

Start short-term—a year, then three, then five, then ten. Focus on the areas of your life that are most important to you, where you want to see meaningful growth and expansion.

Then go through the steps above, honestly and transparently, to build out the foundation—the architecture if you will—for the house you are building for your life. Remember to spare no detail and make sure to dream really big—as this is the house you will live in.

Don't cut any corners. Implement this idea of *Systematic Elevation*, and watch your growth take off in a powerful way.

LET'S GO!

POWER QUOTE

"Planning is bringing the future into the present so that you can do something about it now."

—ALAN LAKEIN

KEY INSIGHT

I view every achievement of each of these goals not as a completion, or a destination, where a goal is accomplished—but rather as simply a new floor.

TACTICAL TIP

Schedule time today to develop a plan for Systematic Elevation where you can plan to achieve what you want.

DAY CHECK

When will you be working on your plan for Systematic Elevation? Is it on your calendar yet? How will you protect that time to develop this plan and execute on it?

COMPASSION

THERE IS A simple elegance and transcendent power to a concept that I think we can all agree is so important in life—compassion.

I am blessed to live in a great country that is fundamentally strong and based solidly on such unyielding principles as liberty, freedom, greatness, opportunity and community.

Because of that, I recognize my unique responsibility to be compassionate to all, a champion of human rights, such as the right to freedom and the opportunity to better the lives of one's family and loved ones.

We must be compassionate and empathetic to people in distress. In times of need, they may be stretched thin, persecuted, or under extreme duress due to political, economic or social pressures.

We have a duty and responsibility to champion these basic human rights and liberties that we often take for granted in a world of hurt, suffering, risk and unfairness.

So, the next time you see a homeless person on the street asking you for money, instead of ignoring them or stopping to give them money that might go to an unworthy cause, suggest a local shelter, or offer a way for them to get a hot meal and some job training.

When you're thinking about donating to that special cause or organization that makes a big difference in the world, instead of just writing a check at the holidays, ask if you can volunteer. Get out and help support them at one of their events or in their daily mission.

When you see wrongs in the world, stand up for what's right and be compassionate to the fact that not everyone comes from the same upbringing and has the same opportunities.

Not everybody starts from the same starting point in this walk or race of life.

We owe it to people to better understand their situation, be compassionate wherever we can to their circumstances and condition and help wherever we are able to in the name of humanity.

LET'S GO!

 POWER QUOTE

"The purpose of human life is to serve and to show compassion and the will to help others."

—ALBERT SCHWEITZER

KEY INSIGHT

So, the next time you see a homeless person on the street asking you for money, instead of ignoring them or stopping to give them money that might go to an unworthy cause, suggest a local shelter or offer a way for them to get a hot meal and some job training.

 ## TACTICAL TIP

Find a way to show compassion around the office or to people you interact with today.

 ## DAY CHECK

How did you go out of your way to show compassion to another person? How did it feel helping someone out?

GROWTH EQUALS PAIN

WITHOUT PAIN, SACRIFICE and some suffering, we will never experience true growth and transformation—to go from where we are to where we want to be.

Growth equals pain. It's that simple.

Only when we push and move outside of our comfort zone and boundaries can we truly adapt and step into our new self-capability.

Consider a simple example from the fitness world. How many times have you had a workout where you push yourself so hard that you literally max out on energy and strength.

Later that day, and the next day in particular, you feel sore, and your muscles hurt because you literally tore cells, stretched and temporarily damaged your muscles.

When muscles undergo intense exercise, there is trauma to the muscle fibers that is actual muscle injury. This disruption to muscle cells activates satellite cells, which are located on the outside of the muscle fibers.

The reason why our muscles grow and our strength grows with commitment and consistency in fitness and weight-training is that, after the stretched or torn cells heal, there are bigger and better cells.

The same concept and process holds true in other areas of life. Think about how much pain comes when trying to take on a new skill and develop that skill. You might be trying to become a better public speaker or learn a new language.

In the beginning, it's hard as you stumble with self-doubt and make mistakes. But then with commitment and consistency, that initial pain turns into growth as you start to build out this new area.

To advance from where we are, we have to have a tolerance for some pain and suffering to get there. Pain can be temporary and fleeting, but deliver extraordinary growth—if we can remain focused on the why behind the effort.

Nothing great ever came without hard work, pain and some adversity. Always remember that when staring down a difficult road to get to where you want to be.

You see, we have to remember that we control the strings that operate ourself and our character in life. We get to decide how we want to move our character and ourself.

If we are unhappy or do not like a quality or a habit in life, we have the ability and freedom to work to change that. If we see that something is detrimental to our growth and our vision, we can work over and through some pain to grow from it, learn and elevate beyond it.

So remember that when things get tough, when we do experience pain and are stretched in an area of our lives, it's not the time to back down, turn and run in the other direction, or find the path of least resistance where the pain will stop immediately.

No. Instead, we need to persevere even if the pain increases in the short run, because when we have a clear destination and know what it takes to get there, only an iron will and the resolve to work through whatever obstacle we encounter will allow us to be successful.

That's what growth is all about—constantly learning, working, improving and being willing to put yourself out there and experience short-term discomfort, unease and pain as you pursue growth, enlightenment and elevation.

LET'S GO!

 ## POWER QUOTE

"Opportunities are usually disguised as hard work, so most people don't recognize them."

—ANN LANDERS

KEY INSIGHT

Nothing great ever came without hard work, pain and some adversity. Always remember that when staring down a difficult road to get to where you want to be.

 ## TACTICAL TIP

What is something that took a lot of hard work to start, but is now easy for you? Imagine if you never did the work. Now, what goals are you stalling on because you're afraid of the hard work? Think about the benefits of your hard work.

 ## DAY CHECK

How did it feel when you finished a hard project or accomplished something that took a lot of effort? What did you accomplish that took determination?

THE DAILY SUCCESS GAME

THERE'S A SIMPLE exercise that has been made into a game that will help keep you healthy, happy and on the right track to achieving your goals.

I want to give proper attribution and credit to a friend and colleague of mine in one of my other businesses named Jay, who shared this with me at our business planning retreat.

This is appropriately entitled *Jay's Eponymous Formula for Success*.

This list of simple daily health habits can help you feel better, healthier, happier and achieve your goals in other areas of your life.

Sometimes it's hard to keep routines, so to make a simple game out of it can help you check things off and stay on track.

So the following is a success planner for daily success. Here's the scorecard:

- *Doing your affirmations, whether they be vocal out loud or written, you will get twenty total points.*

- *Drinking ten 8-ounce glasses of water per day will give you a total of twenty points and a handful of trips to the restroom.*

- *Exercise and sweating at least thirty minutes per day will give you twenty points.*

- *Not complaining at all about anything for the entire day will give you fifteen points.*

- *The simple act of smiling at three people or more each day will give you ten points.*

- *Schedule activities for tomorrow today; meeting success comes from planning tomorrow today. Doing this daily will give you another ten points.*

- *Taking your daily vitamins each day will give you five points.*

So there's a total of 100 possible points here.

Scoring a total of—

- **90- 100 Exceptional**
- **80- 89 Way to go**
- **70- 79 Almost there**
- **60- 69 You can do it**
- **Less than 60 Poor (Get back on track!)**

It is virtually impossible to not accomplish your goals and affirmations if you score 90+ points each day.

So give this a try, and see how small habits and healthy behaviors can be made fun and into a game to stay on track and build consistency.

LET'S GO!

 ## POWER QUOTE

"You have to focus if you want to learn. Keeping your mind on track is essential."

—TONI PAYNE

 ## KEY INSIGHT

Sometimes it's hard to keep routines, so making a simple game out of it can help you check things off and stay on track.

 ## TACTICAL TIP

Try doing the success game for a week and see the difference—or make your own version for the habits you want.

 ## DAY CHECK

How did using a game mindset help you accomplish things today? Did it make it easier?

PRODUCTIVITY HACKS

EVERYBODY LOVES A good list. It's a great way to consume, digest and remember information.

So, I'll share some of my top productivity hacks that I adapted from a fellow entrepreneur named Joel Brown.

The reason why I think these are particularly valuable is that we all face the same dilemma of being as efficient and productive as possible with a limited amount of hours and resources in the day.

As we face increasingly more responsibilities, we become more successful.

Some of these hacks can really help squeeze more from less. I'm always looking for tactics and tips to innovate on time management and productivity.

Here are the top 25 productivity hacks, adapted from fellow entrepreneur Joel Brown:

1. Avoid commuting to the office
2. Learn how to say "No"
3. Do the most important task of the day first

4. Keep your phone in airplane mode until your first task is done
5. Use a set sleep cycle to wake up with energy
6. Exercise in the morning
7. Be goal-oriented rather than following a to-do list
8. Meditate using the Headspace app or other aids
9. Use the Pomodoro technique to manage your time
10. Start the day off using the 60-60-30 technique for productivity
11. Avoid meetings
12. Remember the Pareto Principle (80/20 rule)
13. Avoid eating big meals during the day
14. If it takes less than two minutes, do it now
15. Check email twice a day
16. Tell people to stop distracting you
17. Use background music
18. Plan your day the night before
19. Make 60-second decisions
20. Don't start the day with distraction
21. Make your work environment comfortable
22. Stick to your routine
23. Wake up early to do your morning routine
24. Reward yourself
25. Pick a calendar management tool

Which ones do you already do? Which would help you get more done if you started practicing it today?

Pick a new one and let's get the day started!

LET'S GO!

 ## POWER QUOTE

"No business can succeed in any great degree without being properly organized."

—JAMES CASH PENNEY

 ## KEY INSIGHT

We all face the same dilemma of being as efficient and productive as possible with a limited amount of hours and resources in the day. As we face increasingly more responsibilities, we become more successful.

 ## TACTICAL TIP

Take five things from the list above and act on them for a week, then add some more. Watch how much more productive you feel.

DAY CHECK

What tips helped you today from the list above?

ACCOUNTABILITY LAYERS

I'M SO INCREDIBLY grateful for the opportunity I have—that we all have—to paint the blank canvas of our life as we see fit and realize our vision for our lives and dreams through purposeful action each and every day.

Today I thought it apropos to focus on a key component of whether or not we will actually make our massive vision for our ideal life a reality—or keep it just that, a vision and a dream. That key component is not the strategy or plan, or the action—all of which are critical to this system working.

It is the accountability framework you implement to underpin the entire structure that will determine if the vision actually becomes a reality over time.

We all know the value of accountability; we've discussed it in this section a few times. It is truly foundational for goal achievement. We learned a lot of different things from accountability, and I want to spend a few minutes focusing on accountability best practices and suggestions.

Accountability is best achieved through layers, in my opinion:

- *Superior or mentor*
- *Lateral colleague*

- *Friend*
- *Family member*

Leave the big picture goals and broken-down steps that it will take to get there to your mentor.

Leave the ONE thing that will over time create unstoppable inertia and momentum toward the vision for your accountability partner. You'll need to structure the relationship where you're both helping hold the other person to account for their key action or habit, and doing so honestly and at times, with tough love.

Things to look for in a good partner:

- *Trustworthiness*
- *Positively reinforces, but with tough love*
- *Communicates clearly*
- *Sets schedule, date and time to talk and includes how*
- *Is able to identify the ONE thing—or the Key Metric*

LET'S GO!

 POWER QUOTE

"Accountability is a statement of personal promise, both to yourself and to the people around you, to deliver specific defined results."

—BRIAN DIVE

KEY INSIGHT

Accountability is truly foundational for goal achievement. We learned a lot of different things from accountability.

 ## TACTICAL TIP

Who are some people who hold you accountable? What are ways you can improve the accountability? How can you help be accountable for others?

 ## DAY CHECK

How did you keep yourself accountable today? Who helped you stay accountable on your journey today?

PART FIVE

PEOPLE

*If you treat the people in your life
like your passion, you will immensely
enrich both your life and theirs.*

WE DON'T HAVE anything in this life if we don't have great relationships.

People are everything.

We sometimes lose sight of the people we love the most and who are closest to us by getting too focused on our ambitions and our vision.

Sometimes we need to slow down and take in the moment and our interactions in a more mindful way.

Stay five minutes longer in a conversation with your children. Use your phone for five minutes less. Take a few deep breaths and fill your lungs with oxygen so that you're more alert and aware during a conversation with your significant other.

Little tweaks and changes can make a world of difference in how you interact with people, build trust and rapport, and enhance the relationships that you have with others.

GET THE FREE DOWNLOAD—*7 Frameworks to Live an Inspired Life*—at LiveInspiredBook.com

---

INTENTION 38

TREAT YOUR COLLEAGUES LIKE CLIENTS

W HAT IF WE treated our colleagues, team members
and those we work with the same way we treat our
clients—and we did it by serving them relentlessly and always
helping them achieve their goals?

For instance, in one of my businesses, I've always believed that
real estate brokerages should be structured in a way where
the principal or managing broker isn't involved in sales or production as a competing broker with the agents and associate
brokers within that firm.

The reason behind this, I believe, is that principal brokers and
owners should be treating their agents as the clients. Let the
sales agents in the field treat buyers and sellers as the clients
of the agents, and by extension, clients of the brokerage.

The best model to run a brokerage doesn't lead to conflicts of
interest. Competing skims the best leads and clients from the
top and creates disenfranchisement and disunion between
agents and brokerage.

By treating agents like clients, it also allows the broker to then
be better at providing best-in-market and best-in-class agent
support, training, technology and service so agents can per-

form at a high level. The brokerage can then attract more and more of the best talent in the marketplace.

Now on a team structure, this is a little bit different. The team leader is typically the rainmaker or the highest producer, and the team was formed to support the amount of volume and business the team leader generates and brings in.

Eventually this evolves and grows with time into an ideal, mature team where the team leader is not involved in much of the production, sales or the servicing functions of the team.

It becomes the face, brand equity, and generator of leads with marketing and reputation in the field. Those leads are then distributed to agents on the team to service and work.

With this realization, I learned a very important lesson about the best way for me, as a team leader, to focus my energies.

I'm seeing that by simply laying down a very large vision for the future and career of my entire team, it is not necessarily encompassing nor supportive enough of the individual goals and visions of every member on my team. It is a much broader vision.

I need to spend more time treating each and every one of my team members as my clients, where I'm servicing them and their needs and making sure that they have the best tools, the best marketing, technology and administrative support.

When they win and achieve their goals, the team wins and achieves its goals.

Whether you are on a team or a team leader, this can be a principle and a practice to use with anybody you work with.

When you serve and help others achieve their goals by building their skills, their experience and their confidence, it lifts everybody up around you and will help you achieve your goals in the process.

Remember, we can only drive and take things so far. We're only as good as those around us that we build up and help grow as well.

Spend time focusing on ways in which you can better serve your colleagues and those that you work with in the same fashion, and ways that we serve the interests and the goals of our clients and customers.

When we do this we will truly create a culture of reciprocity, mutual benefit, loyalty and growth that we would not be able to achieve otherwise.

LET'S GO!

 POWER QUOTE

"Never lose sight of the fact that the most important yard-stick of your success will be how you treat people - your family, friends, and coworkers, and even strangers you meet along the way."

—BARBARA BUSH

KEY INSIGHT

I'm realizing I need to spend more time treating each and every one of my team members as my clients as well, where I'm servicing them and their needs and making sure that they have the best tools, the best marketing, technology and administrative support, so that they can achieve their goals. When they win and achieve their goals, the company wins and achieves its goals.

TACTICAL TIP

How are you empowering the people around you? Are you doing everything you can to give your team or colleagues what they need to achieve their goals?

DAY CHECK

How did you empower someone today? What did you do that helped someone else accomplish a goal?

DEEP FRIENDSHIPS

HOW IMPORTANT IS it to create and foster deep friendships and relationships with the right people in life?

I'm sure everyone can relate to the fact that as we get older and busier with families and increasingly demanding schedules, it becomes difficult to maintain as many friendships as we once did, and to do so in any meaningful way.

Friendships and relationships take effort, energy, time and emotion to maintain, develop and keep alive. If we don't actively invest in them, they can often resemble a living organism or a plant.

If we're not watering it, giving it nutrients and maintaining it, it can fade and falter.

As we grow older, our friendships with people in our lives will change. Some will fall, and we may even consciously make decisions not to spend time with people that aren't growing in the same direction as we are.

Being around certain people might become negative and even toxic in our lives. In that case, it's imperative that we realize we can't change them, but we'll need to spend far less time around them or even remove them from our lives because of the negative impact it has.

The number of people who you become close friends with will start to shrink and firm up, and the more adversity or things that we go through and experience in our journey, the more clearly we'll see who our true and genuine friends really are.

This is entirely okay.

We need to remember and accept that it's not about how many people that we stay in touch with regularly, but it's rather the quality of these relationships and friendships that we deliberately choose to invest in that really makes a difference.

I'm finding it increasingly difficult to maintain the level of engagement with many of my older friends as I once had simply due to how busy I have become.

However, I have been very up front and honest about this with my friends, and they understand that I am in laser-focused, hyper-growth mode and really trying to build something great here in the world with a huge vision and tenacious commitment.

Life has seasons and sacrifices. The key is balancing everything to meet your priorities and values.

What's remarkable is that I have many friends that, although we might not see each other or talk on the phone as much as we might like, no matter how much time elapses when we get back together, it's like we never missed a beat. It's right back to where we were last time.

The level of rapport, connectedness and just the enjoyment of each other's company and the fun that we've always had is so real and strong that it stands up to the test of time. It doesn't necessarily fade or lessen with distance and time apart.

Today I want to challenge you to take time to invest in doing a bit of an audit on your friendships and the people you deliberately place and allow into your life.

Remember, we want to always ensure that these people are having a positive effect on our life experience, and that we're able to contribute and have a positive effect on theirs as well, in a supportive and mutually-beneficial friendship.

If these things aren't true, it's important to take swift action and accept that sometimes things change in life. Sometimes things can't be forced in the name of friendship or because of history that you might have.

It's okay to do that.

It's okay to remove yourself and be very focused on the short list of people you are going to invest your time and energy in, the people with whom you are going to maintain a friendship and relationship.

This is important, as friendships and relationships are all about reciprocity and mutual uplift. If that's not there, and if things have changed or evolved, that's okay, but we need to recognize it.

LET'S GO!

 ## POWER QUOTE

"When you choose your friends, don't be short-changed by choosing personality over character."

—W. SOMERSET MAUGHAM

 ## KEY INSIGHT

It's not about how many people that we stay in touch with regularly, but it's rather the quality of these relationships and friendships that we deliberately choose to invest in that really makes a difference.

 ## TACTICAL TIP

Who are your closest friends? Do you lift each other up or tear each other down? Is your relationship built on trust and honesty, or drama and pain? Try making a list of your friends and writing down key words that describe your relationship with each person and see what comes up.

 ## DAY CHECK

Did you reach out to someone today? How did you build on a healthy friendship today?

INVESTING IN FAMILY

LET'S FOCUS TODAY on the importance of investing and making sure that we are always making time to be there for our family. Let's ensure that we create opportunities to build lifelong memories with them and never become too busy to do so.

I think today, more than ever, we're all so busy that it really requires diligence and focus to schedule and create meaningful time that we can spend with our families. This is particularly true as our busy schedules conflict because of family, careers and other responsibilities.

I have one brother who is five years younger than me and has two young children. His name is Jared. We've always been super close growing up, even though we're five years apart.

One of the things that I am extremely grateful for is a childhood in which I was fortunate to have amazing parents and an amazing younger brother who I can still call a best friend today, even as adults.

I also know that this isn't always the case, and siblings don't always get along. Sometimes as they grow older, they fall less and less in touch, can become distant and, in certain cases, not even talk to one another.

I find this to be very hard to comprehend and think it's unfortunate when this happens—but I understand that it does.

My brother and I talk pretty much every day. I see him as often as I can, which is more difficult now that he lives in Virginia and we are both extremely busy.

I thought it would be a really great gift to give him a ticket to a very special event that I was attending in Southern California. The entire event was focused on designing your perfect life and career and building it to match your vision, but doing it in a way that places high ambition in harmony with a high quality of life and experience.

We flew out a little bit ahead of time, rented a fun, fast car and drove up the Pacific Coast Highway to explore California and areas that he'd never visited. I couldn't have been more excited to spend some quality time with my younger brother.

I wanted to really connect and build on our friendship and relationship on this mini-vacation, capped off and followed by the privilege of attending an amazing event in San Diego at the end of the week.

The reason why I'm sharing this is that it's really important that we realize how short life really is and how important our relationships are with our family members, particularly our siblings.

To develop a sibling relationship into a friendship takes work, commitment and getting over differences in personality and approaches to life that may have caused divisions or conflicts in childhood growing up.

But life is really short, and I find it tragic when I see siblings don't talk at all due to differences in opinion or their outlook as adults.

So I want to encourage everyone, whether you have a good relationship, okay relationship, or no relationship with your siblings or maybe another family member that you've fallen out of touch with, take the time today, this week, to reach out.

Take the time to tell them that you've been thinking about them and that you hope they're doing well, that you're here for them and that you'd like to see them. Then start small and schedule a phone call to catch up.

Perhaps you could build from a phone call into a time when you can get together and really connect, bond and catch up.

Even if there was an event or something that really put a divide between you, the worst thing that can happen is living with the regret and the wonder of a relationship that could have been.

Neither of my parents had very close relationships with either of their siblings, and I watched the effect that had on them and the family, so I committed to never letting that happen with my younger brother.

I'm happy, proud and grateful that we have the friendship we have, and I'm going to continue to invest in that and do the work it takes to keep that healthy.

LET'S GO!

 ## POWER QUOTE

"The family is the center of life, and it is the key to eternal happiness."

—L. TOM PERRY

 ## KEY INSIGHT

I think today, more than ever, we're all so busy that it really requires diligence and focus to schedule in and create meaningful time that we can spend with our families and our siblings, particularly as our busy schedules conflict because of family, careers and other responsibilities.

 ## TACTICAL TIP

Call your parents, siblings, cousins—any relative that you are close to—and reconnect. If you don't have family, call a close friend and connect with them.

 ## DAY CHECK

Who did you reconnect with today? How did it feel to talk to someone you feel a connection with?

PROXIMITY IS POWER

I ONCE TOOK A two-week-long trip attending three conferences in a row: First, speaking at an industry event in San Francisco, followed by a summit in Las Vegas, followed by the Tony Robbins Business Mastery event in Las Vegas.

That's a long time to be away from home and businesses, but it was such an amazing experience to be at all three of these back-to-back. The teachings, takeaways, relationships—both new connections and old friends—were absolutely extraordinary.

I believe strongly in constant personal and professional development, improving your mind, body and spirit and investing time, money and effort into becoming the best person and professional that you can possibly be.

This is also a culture I've created for my teams in the businesses I own. I want to focus on some key takeaways I learned and brought home with me from my travels to these conferences, with several coming from Tony Robbins at his Business Mastery five-day retreat. I would highly recommend attending one of his events if you can. It's really transformative if you're open to it.

Tony Robbins has been a huge idol of mine for years, as I think he is the world's leading expert on self-improvement and mastery and is hugely inspirational.

I started coaching with the Tony Robbins organization and purchased the Business Mastery event ticket. With it, came a UPW (Unleash the Power Within) ticket, as well. I learned the hard way that nothing is "free" when I didn't upgrade my seating, finding myself in the nosebleed section far away from the stage where Tony was presenting and inspiring over 14,000 people!

I learned my lesson there, and made sure I upgraded so I could be in the front row no matter what it cost at Business Mastery.

Because proximity is power, in life and in business. Remember that, *proximity is power.*

You are a reflection of those people you spend the most time with and associate with, and your net worth is a reflection of the average of those same people. This is so fundamentally true. So, there we are starting this intensive course with Tony teaching it himself. I'm sitting smack in the front row, high fiving him, talking with Tony and connecting with him and other amazing people from across the world who are passionate and committed to their success and happiness at a very high level.

Some of the people I find myself surrounded with include but are not limited to: close personal friends of Tony Robbins himself, highly successful business executives, and business owners from all sorts of industries and from all over.

There was a world-renowned architect for the super wealthy who builds $30M estates around the world; she needed a marketing partner to help her clients find and sell these estates once they were ready.

This was just one example of the many people I met.

The relationships and the people I met, the business opportunities that were formed, and the exposure to growth professionally and personally, all came as a result of my proximity to the right people.

Had I not invested the money to go to the event, invested the money to upgrade so I could be close to Tony and the most committed people up front, had I not networked like crazy, I would not have met these world-class people.

Proximity is power.

Find a role model or role models for areas in your life in which you want to improve, grow and advance. This could be career, family, financially, etc.

Find those people who are doing it and crushing it, and find a way to connect with them. Model their behavior, learn from their failures, be around their successes.

Proximity is power, and we must put this into action and identify, make a plan to connect and model and then be accountable to ourselves and to our plan to see it through to the end.

Decide where you want to go and who you want to become. Dream big, put yourself around those much further than you, find mentors and role models, model their behavior, their successes and their path.

Never take no for an answer, and don't be scared or intimidated by what you think you can't achieve.

I am a firm believer that what the mind can dream and believe, it can achieve.

LET'S GO!

POWER QUOTE

"Pick your role models wisely, find out what they did and do it."

—LANA DEL REY

KEY INSIGHT

Proximity is power, in life and in business. Remember that, proximity is power. You are a reflection of those people you spend the most time with and associate with, and your net worth is a reflection of the average of those same people. This is so fundamentally true.

TACTICAL TIP

Who are your role models? Have you ever wondered how they got to where they are? Do some research on people you admire and look up to, then look at the struggles they went through and how they endured.

DAY CHECK

How did you learn from your role model? What mindset or action did you copy from someone you admire?

INTENTION 42

ADVOCATE FOR YOUR CUSTOMER

S O THE CONCEPT I want to focus on today is the idea of defending and advocating for our clients' or customers' interests—no matter what.

Let's think about this for a minute. This is not focusing on our skills and career building; it's not focusing on just closing a deal for a sale or a client; it doesn't matter what we are selling or who we serve in business or life—it's the idea of rigorously and unapologetically defending the interests of those we serve.

No excuses.

It's advocating for their best interests and their goals, wishes, dreams and desires. It's knowing their fears and apprehensions better than they do, and speaking to them in a way that makes them feel safe before they know they are in danger.

When we do this, consistently, it changes the game and elevates the level of service, success and experience of those that we serve and come into contact with in our businesses and in life.

So we need to be both the protector of our client and also the promoter. We need to guard and defend against their fears, and we need to promote and advocate for their dreams and desires.

When we do these things, we serve at the highest level. We lead at an extraordinary level. We deliver value at an unparalleled level.

We create experiences and results that are so appreciated, novel and unique—they have the opportunity to actually transform and change lives.

When we do that successfully, there is NO better feeling. None. Do you know what happens next?

Our practice catches and grows like wildfire. Now our clients and those we serve are not just numbers in the machine we call business, brokerage, coaching or sales—whatever it is we are selling.

Now they become raving, loving, appreciative fans and ambassadors of our brand. Of you. Of me. Of us. Of what you stand for and what you deliver.

This is the best feeling in the world, and it will lead to multiplying opportunities to repeat this and deliver and serve at a level you've previously not been able to, which results in client experiences and results previously unattained.

So let's go out today and this week, and start by putting our clients and customers, those we serve, ahead of all else. We need to start defending and advocating for them rigorously above all else. This is our charge and our duty; this is the mandate.

Go out, and if you do nothing else, make sure you defend and advocate tirelessly—never let up and never let this part of your practice, business, brand, legacy and life—be sacrificed for anything.

LET'S GO!

 ## POWER QUOTE

"The golden rule for every business(person) is this: Put yourself in your customer's place."

—ORISON SWETT MARDEN

 ## KEY INSIGHT

We need to be both the protector of our client, and also the promoter. We need to guard and defend against their fears, and we need to promote and advocate for their dreams and desires.

When we do these things, we serve at the highest level. We lead at an extraordinary level. We deliver value at an unparalleled level. We create experiences and results that are so appreciated, novel and unique—they have the opportunity to actually transform and change lives.

TACTICAL TIP

Put yourself into the clients' mind. Whatever your goal audience is, you need to think like them and give them what they want in a way that benefits you. But when you put the client before yourself, that gives your work a touch that is unique and sincere. People will always come back and share things that are genuine.

 ## DAY CHECK

How did you put your audience before yourself today? How did you stretch your mind to think like someone else?

STRATEGIC RELATIONSHIPS

I **WANT TO DISCUSS** the importance of forming strong and strategic relationships and partnerships to achieve our goals.

The unique ability that we have in this business of relationships is identifying and pursuing opportunities; some come our way, or we might discover others through our interactions with so many different people of different backgrounds, careers and experiences.

In order to do this, a few things are critical. One, we have to start by building rapport and trust from the first time we meet someone.

We do that by demonstrating knowledge and expertise in our field and in what we are talking about, the reason why we are there in the first place.

Then we establish common ground or things that we both partake in, value or enjoy that we can discuss and bond over.

We also want to find and identify the one or two things that are most important to the other person and see if there are ways in which we can help support them in achieving whatever that is.

We have to always start by asking how can we deliver value and support to someone else in their pursuit of their goals, whatever they may be.

Once we do this, a relationship is born that is not simply transactional in nature, but can be reciprocal and symbiotic in form.

When we support others and what they're trying to achieve in their important projects and larger "why", they naturally want to support us in the pursuit of our goals and put us in touch with the right people that will help us to that end.

The old Golden Rule of networking goes, "Always give and add value before ever asking for something of anyone."

Now we have to start looking at forming these relationships and friendships with the people that we interact with on a daily basis, including clients.

With the right investment of time and effort, clients can potentially become our friends, business partners or even connect us to new partners, investments, ideas and things that will help support us in our vision and our growth.

Let's start looking at these relationships not just as transactional in nature, but as strategic opportunities for growth for the other person and also for you.

This is how we advance and elevate in a win-win, mutually beneficial way.

LET'S GO!

POWER QUOTE

"Business is all about relationships—how well you build them determines how well they build your business."

—BRAD SUGARS

KEY INSIGHT

Focus on the quality of the relationships we are forming with the people that we come across and meet in our career and in our lives. Let's start looking at these relationships not just as transactional in nature, but as strategic opportunities for growth for the other person and also for you. This is how we advance and elevate in a win-win mutually beneficial way.

TACTICAL TIP

When you show people that you are interested in their dreams, they are more prone to help you with your dreams. Try helping others out as you go about your day, without expecting anything in return. Help your coworkers and others that you interact with daily.

 **DAY CHECK**

How did you help someone achieve their dream today? How did the person react to your enthusiasm to help?

GROWING RELATIONSHIPS

TODAY I WANT to address the importance of creating and maintaining healthy friendships and relationships people that you surround yourself with in life.

This is absolutely critical. If we are not surrounding ourselves with positive, like-minded people who add to and enrich our lives, who support us and our goals, then we can fall into a regressive state and have our minds severely compromised. This can happen simply by being around the wrong people.

I'm sure all of us have had those friends or people in our lives that require a lot of energy, support or are just plain pessimistic or negative to a point where spending time with them does not uplift or inspire at all.

It's actually the opposite; it can be very detrimental. Whether this is an old high-school friend, a family friend or even a family member, it's really important we identify those people around us that are having a negative impact on us.

We need to take action to help them improve their mindset and approach while recognizing and knowing that it's not easy to adjust. And if someone doesn't want to change, it's not our obligation, nor are we responsible for it.

What we are responsible for is keeping ourselves and our family safe and healthy.

As hard as that is, sometimes it requires us to remove certain people from our lives, or at least limit the amount of time and influence they have on our lives.

What we really need to do is double down and spend more time investing in growing our relationships with those people who really contribute to and enrich our lives. We need to make sure they know how much they are appreciated.

We need to spend more time building our bonds and our relationships with people that build us up, support and encourage us—people with good character and constitution that we can benefit from being around and who can benefit from us.

Try to be more mindful of the people we have in our lives, who we deliberately choose to be around. We have the freedom to choose those we spend time with, for how long and for what reason.

Let's make a conscious effort to identify relationships and friendships that are having a negative impact on our psyche and our lives, and slowly remove them. We need to take care of ourselves first, to make sure that we are healthy and strong, before we can be at our best to support our family, friends or colleagues.

People with bad attitudes and worldviews can be detrimental and insidious, and we need to guard against that.

We need to slow down a little bit sometimes, appreciate and take everything in and make sure that we're giving enough time to relax and enjoy life and the journey that we are all on.

Sometimes time gets sacrificed when you are very ambitious and have a high vision for life. If we don't commit and spend the time maintaining the relationships with those that we love, care for and respect, then they will suffer and not always necessarily be there.

We do not want to regret this later, and it can happen easily if we don't pay attention regularly.

LET'S GO!

 ## POWER QUOTE

"Don't let negative and toxic people rent space in your head... raise the rent and kick them out."

—ROBERT TEW

 ## KEY INSIGHT

What we really need to do is double down and spend more time investing in growing our relationships with those people who really contribute to and enrich our lives. We need to make sure they know how much they are appreciated.

TACTICAL TIP

Think about the people you have in your life. Which ones make you feel exhausted after a conversation, and which ones build you up? As you interact with people, think about how they affect your life.

 DAY CHECK

What did you notice about your relationships today? Who are some people who are positive influences? Which ones are negative?

MAKE TIME COUNT!

I WENT THROUGH A very difficult process when we sold my childhood home, the home that I grew up in and my father's favorite place in the world.

It was not an easy thing to do, as I had so many memories made there while growing up. The property had been in our family for over twenty years.

It's funny how a place can mean so much, even though it's just a physical place in the world. However, we can take those memories, experiences, love and the things that were created wherever we go.

I remember going through the items at the house, deciding what to keep, what was going where, who was going to get what and all the other things that you typically do before you sell a home.

I came across many old pictures, letters and keepsakes from growing up. It's amazing how good my hair looked at one point, but the size of my jeans was ridiculous during the skater phase in middle school!

It was a very emotional process as my family and I were detaching and disengaging from our old home. My father passed away in this house a few years prior, which made it even harder to let go.

My father was my best friend and the most amazing person I've ever met. He was a man of such integrity, compassion and charisma—all of the values that you look for in a father, a leader and a mentor. I miss my dad each and every day, but his memory and legacy endures and lives on.

As I was going through some old boxes, I found a box with a bunch of letters from when I was in prison for a tragic boat accident. There were letters from friends, my core group from high school, my mother and my brother.

There were the regular letters from my father too. He was my biggest supporter, even when I didn't deserve one.

As I was going through his letters, I found a card that he had sent me shortly after I had been faced with the denial of being released. I was completely dejected and distraught for a few weeks, not knowing how I was going to muster the courage to face things and move on so I could make it through.

I found the card and the message that my dad sent me at that critical juncture in my life, and I was immediately floored emotionally. The card said...

"Don't count time, make time count."

Wow! Powerful!!

Think about that for a minute. Time is such an interesting concept, it is finite and our most valuable resource. It is something we judge things in our lives against, and I was just simply waiting.

I was counting the days, minutes and seconds until I was going to be able to essentially start over and have a new chance and lease on life. I wanted to do something different, special and purposeful with my life.

But that wasn't the right way of looking at it. My dad made me able to understand this. You see, we have a unique ability, no matter where we are or what circumstances we face or how hard our current situation is, to seize the opportunity and make the most of our current circumstances with positivity, purpose and gratitude, no matter how difficult or bleak our circumstances are.

There are people across the world who live in such poverty that it can make you sick to your stomach to see how they live.

However, some of these very people are the happiest in the world. They have chosen the mindset of being present, loving and supportive of their family despite the circumstances.

Don't count time, make time count.

I took this encouragement and this wisdom for my father and ran with it. I doubled down on my inner workings and focused on growing as much as I could while I was away.

I wanted to be in the best health of my life, physically, mentally, emotionally and spiritually.

So I want to leave you with this thought and lesson today. Let's not count down the days, let's not gauge our goals simply on the spectrum of time. Let's stop counting down the days until we will be *happy*, until we will be *successful*, thinking if we just hit these goals the rest of the world will fall into place for us.

Stop doing all of that, and let's simply make time count and work for us, putting every bit of energy, focus and determination into the moments that we're so fortunate to have on this earth.

Let's not take any moment, day or opportunity for granted. Let's tell the people that we love we love them more and more each day, and let's make sure they know and never forget.

Let's put purpose and meaning back into our actions in our lives, rather than sometimes simply walking through them vacantly.

LET'S GO!

 ## POWER QUOTE

"Don't count time, make time count!"

—MARK WEIMER (1949-2016)

 ## KEY INSIGHT

The card said ... Don't count time, make time count. Wow! Powerful. Think about that for a minute. Time is such an interesting concept, more finite and a valuable resource. It is something we judge things in our lives against, and I was just simply waiting.

TACTICAL TIP

Take time today to tell the ones you love how much you appreciate them. Think about a world where the ones you love most are gone. How would you feel? Every moment counts with the ones you love.

 ## DAY CHECK

Who did you show how much you love them? How did you make time count today?

EMBRACE THE MOMENTS

I LOVE THE CHRISTMAS holiday season. Even for those who do not celebrate Christmas, it's still a great time at the end of the year to reflect on all we have to be grateful for—the people and relationships in our lives that we value, the abundance we've created, our health, and achievements in other areas of our lives.

We have so much to be grateful for. I live in a great country of freedom, opportunity and liberty to pursue our dreams, happiness and what we were meant to do in this world.

We all have a better chance and a better opportunity now than we ever have in the entire history of the world to do this—right now, right here, at this very moment in time.

But it's important that we don't forget a few things. We get so focused on our goals, vision and achieving the things that are important to us, we sometimes lose track of the present, the very reason why we work so hard.

We try to create a better quality of life for ourselves and for those people that we love, honor and respect in this world.

Think about it for a minute: it all boils down to us working to elevate our quality of life and our experience in this world. If we work too hard, then we never get to really sit back and enjoy the increases and gains we've made to that end.

We wind up asking, "What is it all for, anyway?"

We need to recognize that the moments and special times are fleeting. Make an effort to capture the very essence of humanity and life in these moments.

This could be watching the snow fall slowly through the air and observing the uniqueness of creation. Or it could be helping somebody who needs a hand carrying in wood for a fire or doing something nice for a stranger.

Recently I picked up the bill for an old man eating alone. I did it without him ever knowing. These are the things that make life worth living, the small moments of joy, love, happiness and of helping other people get to the same place we're trying to get to, which is a better quality of life and a better experience as humans in this world.

So, no matter the time of year, let's try to take in each and every moment, to be especially present with our family, friends and those that we get to spend time with.

Let us try to detach from devices and contribute to and absorb all that is around us. We have so much to be grateful for, and we are so fortunate to have this opportunity in life.

Let's make sure that life doesn't pass us by while we're too focused and working too hard on trying to realize the life that we don't have. We will end up neglecting the invaluable moments that we do have each and every day.

Life is fragile, short and impermanent; let's make the best of it one moment at a time.

LET'S GO!

 ## POWER QUOTE

"I'm thankful for every moment."

—AL GREEN

 ## KEY INSIGHT

Let us try and really detach from devices and really contribute and absorb all that is around us. We have so much to be grateful for, and we are so fortunate to have this opportunity in life. Let's make sure that life doesn't pass us by while we're too focused and working too hard on trying to realize the life that we don't have. We will end up neglecting the invaluable moments that we do have each and every day.

 ## TACTICAL TIP

Take some time today and reflect on all your blessings. Think about how privileged you are to have what you have. Why should we only be thankful on holidays for what we have? Every day we should take time to be thankful for what we have and the opportunities we are blessed with.

DAY CHECK

What small moments happened today that you should be thankful for? How does it feel to reflect on the day looking for the small joys?

PART SIX

LEADERSHIP

To effectively lead and inspire others, always strive to be the best version of yourself.

LEADERSHIP IS NOT an easy science or practice. Leading others through example, persuasion, shared values and mission is challenging. You have to create a culture of buy-in, and there has to be shared values and commonality in purpose, mission and vision. There has to be humility and circumspection on the part of the leader in order to be truly effective.

In order to be an effective leader, it's important to embrace and live the very values you espouse and encourage others to live by. The example we set through our actions and our values is much stronger and more influential than any words we may speak. Let us work to align our daily actions and intentions with our values and our vision no matter what line of work or area of life requires our leadership.

When we are driven by a desire to grow and build community, with a focus on creating a culture of transparency and accountability, then we will have fertile ground to lead others to greatness and to do so with commonality and singularity of purpose and mission.

GET THE FREE DOWNLOAD—*7 Frameworks to Live an Inspired Life*—*at LiveInspiredBook.com*

CULTURE

I WANT TO TALK about something that impacts all of us in many ways. It's something that is not unique to our businesses, and its value is not limited to only one area of our lives. This is something that forms the basis from which we operate, both professionally and personally.

This is the foundation of what we do and what we create—*culture*.

I also want to tie in the concept and importance of energy and enthusiasm, and the massive impact this can have on our lives. The inspiration for this is derived from two books that I have read: *Daring Greatly* and *The Energy Bus*.

Merriam-Webster defines culture as "the set of shared attitudes, values, goals and practices that characterizes an institution, organization or group."

We create cultures from our mission statement, values, behaviors and judgments. Culture forms the bedrock from which we act in this world. Without culture, there is no fabric holding it all together.

Culture is a type of glue that binds together the beliefs, values and goals of a group of like-minded people.

In the business world, there's an ongoing debate about the relationship between strategy and culture, and the relative importance of each.

Just to define the terms, strategy is "the game plan" or the detailed answer to the question, "What do we want to achieve, and how are we going to get there?"

All of us—families, religious groups, project teams and teachers—have game plans.

We all think about the goals we want to accomplish and the steps we need to take to be successful. In fact, we spend a lot of time on this in coaching and in our businesses.

Culture, on the other hand, is less about what we want to achieve and more about who we are.

Our WHY.

It's what drives us and binds us together, working for the same end and purpose.

I would argue that culture is just as important, if not more important, than strategy.

So, *what is your work culture like?*

Have you defined your work culture and are you working on it constantly?

Is it genuine and transparent, and does everyone know what it is? Do they not only buy into it, but contribute to it while also benefiting from it?

Asking ourselves what our work culture is like could be one of the most important questions we consider—culture is really everything.

It's the essence of our character, our environment, the ethos, if you will, and it can mean the difference between success and failure.

LET'S GO!

 ## POWER QUOTE

"Every man's ability may be strengthened or increased by culture."

—JOHN ABBOT

 ## KEY INSIGHT

I would argue that culture is just as important, if not more important, than strategy. It's what drives us and binds us together, working for the same end and purpose.

 ## TACTICAL TIP

What is your work culture like? Have you defined your work culture, and are you working on it constantly? Think of different work cultures you have experienced, and compare them to your current situation.

DAY CHECK

How did the way you defined your culture and the way you experienced it today differ? Is your culture uplifting or detracting?

BEDROCK OF CULTURE

WHAT USUALLY FORMS the bedrock of culture is the vision, mission statement and values that we have chosen to represent and guide us.

Culture cannot be a decree or distilled to a simple saying or value statement on a whiteboard.

While those things are important, culture is really formed through behaviors, beliefs and community.

How many times have we been told that in order to connect and lead, we should show and not tell?

I've always grappled with this in my writing, as I tend to want to explain and describe things more than I want to show or tell to illustrate my point.

That's how the best stories are written, the most effective messages delivered and how the most successful people create powerful, fun and transformative cultures.

Value alignment is critical to creating a strong culture, and one that is genuinely authentic creates an environment that is ripe for growth. When writing our team value statement, I found it important to focus on verbs, not just static nouns or things unrelatable. Many companies have value and mission statements, but don't end up creating powerful and rewarding cultures.

This is because they are not owning their values, embracing them and making them ingrained in their behavior and day-to-day approach to the business.

Wells Fargo. Everyone remembers this, right? The fake account scandal.

This banking behemoth became a culture of short-term results with a monthly and quarterly focus on signing up new accounts. They made driving quotas and the bottom lines a priority over focusing on delivering great products and services for their clients.

We all know what happened after this. It led to complete collapse and imploding.

The culture had gone very quickly awry. Billions of dollars were lost, and thousands of employees were fired. Total failure. Now, let's think about what might have happened if the senior management had created a culture centered on delivering the best products and services to their clients.

What if they had focused on being great at what they do, setting themselves apart from their peers and growing and gaining market share?

Well, had they done that, they might have become the largest bank in the U.S. with a stellar reputation. They would have hundreds of thousands of happy clients recommending them to family, friends and loads of potential new customers.

Unfortunately, however, their culture became focused on results and results only, where the end justifies the means.

Management failed, and employees failed, all because of a bad culture.

One of the many things I've learned in my career and life is that if you focus on being really great at what you do, and outperform your competitors instead of focusing on the money, fame or glory of success, then you will be far more successful, happy and looked up to.

When you are great and can create a culture of greatness—everything else will follow, and so, too, will the trappings of success.

LET'S GO!

 ## POWER QUOTE

"There's never a point where you can stop getting better."

—KEVIN DURANT

 ## KEY INSIGHT

When you are great and can create a culture of greatness—everything else will follow, and so, too, will the trappings of success.

TACTICAL TIP

Think about the focus of your life or business. What are you centered on? Are you focused on being the greatest, or on just being successful?

 ## DAY CHECK

What did you notice about your work culture today? Was it uplifting? Was it focused on delivering and serving, or on making money achieving success?

GREATNESS

THE RIGHT CULTURE, one that is empowering, collaborative, fun, engaging and effective, can lead to true Greatness. Greatness is a pretty significant word—one of the biggest in the sense of whether it can even be quantified. When has greatness been achieved?

Greatness is a concept and a school of study, thought and discipline that countless scholars over time have explored and have tried to understand why some ideas, people and cultures rise to greatness—while others lag or even fall to destruction.

Greatness can be thought of as being distinguished, remarkable, exceptional and outstanding. This can come in many forms and on many different levels or magnitudes.

What I have done in my life, at the request of my coach, and carried over to transcend to my team and my other businesses, is distill all of my values, strategies, mission statements, business plans and fancy systems, into one word.

This was a very difficult process for me. As someone who is long-winded and verbose, I like words and would rather wax poetic than leave things open to interpretation or the imagination. So, I did this exercise after finishing all of my business and team planning documents. It was exhausting, as I handed in almost one-hundred pages for our Mastermind group to review.

I'm pretty sure everyone just read the Executive Summary. This is not to say planning and the mechanics of a well-oiled team are unimportant, quite the contrary.

But culture is more important.

Mindset is also more important in my opinion. And our WHY is more important. So, after all of this, I came to the realization that my one word is *greatness*.

Put simply, I will not rest; I will not stop working on any given day, on any given project, in any given business, in any given year—until I know I couldn't have done it any better.

When I have given one-hundred-thirty percent to my family, friends, team, colleagues, clients, everyone in my life and everything in my life, I am free.

I am at peace.

I have arrived at a state of calm and a peaceful mind, knowing that my *greatness* has been achieved. When this is reflected and observed by others, this serves as an affirmation of what I'm doing and that I'm doing the right thing. In a business sense, I do make sure I'm more prepared than anyone in the market by...

- *knowing more about the markets we are in,*
- *having best in class marketing and technology,*

- *providing our clients with the best, most memorable white-glove experience they've ever had,*
- *having a winning attitude,*
- *envisioning the result I seek, and*
- *putting in the work to be great at the task at hand.*

If I can do that, the money, acclaim, recognition and everything else follows.

Lead with greatness and merit in this world, and I have found you will be handsomely rewarded by the forces that be in the universe. What I'd like to ask you to do is to spend some time and think about your culture. Think about your culture at home, work, etc.

Think about where things could be improved, where there might be areas of growth, how sometimes small tweaks and changes over time can lead to massive shifts in culture and results.

Just think how transformative this would be with just a five minute commitment to our morning to set the table and the tone for the day, and provide a foundation for *greatness*.

Some principles I've found beneficial in creating a durable and successful culture on my team and inspiring others to seek and achieve *greatness* include:

1. Make time for others.
2. Listen to them.
3. Recognize hard work and results regularly.

4. Serve your employees and partners. Give first before you ever ask.

5. Bring out the best in them by supporting, encouraging and inspiring them with the example you lead in behavior.

6. Challenge and stimulate your employees through adding responsibilities and accountability.

7. Go on at least two retreats or days off together as a team. Work on the business. More importantly, have fun and build your team.

8. Lead by example.

LET'S GO!

 ## POWER QUOTE

"You can have all the right strategies in the world; if you don't have the right culture, you're dead."

—PATRICK WHITESELL

 ## KEY INSIGHT

Lead with greatness and merit in this world, and I have found you will be handsomely rewarded by the forces that be in the universe.

TACTICAL TIP

Try implementing three of the principles above today and see how it affects your culture.

DAY CHECK

How did the principles affect your day and culture? Did you see any big changes or improvements?

INTENTION 50

GOOD LEADERSHIP

I WANT TO START by giving some historical context to the concept of leadership, and how our environment can influence our type and style of leadership, as well as how effective and transformative it can be—or how destructive and oppressive the wrong type of leadership can be. Leadership has many different definitions for many different people, depending on what perspective you're coming from.

When we think of leadership in the traditional sense, we may think of someone who leads others. Or it might be someone who simply has followers, manages or oversees. But this is a dated and transactional definition of leadership that is quite limited. Our friends at Merriam Webster define leadership as: "The ability to lead or mold individuals into a team."

I feel leadership is so much more than this. When I think of leadership, I think of:

- *The ability to inspire and move people to action first and foremost*
- *The ability to generate social influence*
- *The ability to behave and act in a way that attracts others*

- *The ability to create, grow and sustain a group of people based on common values, beliefs and goals*
- *Creating an environment that is conducive to growth*
- *Empowering others to achieve their goals and realize their dreams*
- *Turning vision into reality*
- *Having confidence and clarity of purpose*
- *Having integrity and making your word your law, meaning do what you say you're going to do, and do it when you say you're going to do it*
- *Being reliable, approachable, coachable and humble*
- *Doing the right thing always, especially when no one is watching*
- *Being accountable to yourself and to others*
- *Always having a growth mindset and not a fixed mindset*
- *Looking for the good in everything, being open to life's teaching moments, and being able to identify opportunities in the unlikeliest of circumstances*
- *Actively listening, responding, being empathetic and identifying and relating to the needs, wants and goals of those in the group*

When leaders broaden their definition and capacity to comprehend the concept of leadership and all that it entails, leadership turns into a whole new mission, an undertaking that puts *others* first.

Think about that. Others first.

The idea is that what you do has a direct impact on the lives and well-being of others, not only recognizing the gravity and weight of this charge, but embracing it and making it the duty of the leader to serve—and never to be served.

When a leader heads down the path of entitlement, feeling like they and their needs must be met and served by the group, that is the moment when leadership fails. Good leadership, at its core, is a concept based on the principles of democracy and meritocracy.

You might ask why this is the case. It's because good leaders, like good ideas and political solutions, rise on their merits. They rise because they attract people to the group through the value they offer to them and the world.

It's about the culture they're creating.

Does it promote and support the shared values and beliefs of the individuals in the group? Is it a fertile environment where creativity, new ideas, innovation and risk-taking is encouraged?

If it is, then leadership has succeeded. Leadership succeeds through attraction, not promotion. Through merits, not orders. Through inspiration, not mandate.

LET'S GO!

 ## POWER QUOTE

"A leader is one who knows the way, goes the way, and shows the way."

—JOHN C. MAXWELL

 ## KEY INSIGHT

Leadership succeeds through attraction, not promotion. Through merits, not orders. Through inspiration, not mandate.

 ## TACTICAL TIP

What are your core principles of democracy and meritocracy? Do you share values with those you lead? Make a point today to listen to others so you may better lead them.

 ## DAY CHECK

What people under your leadership differ with your values, and who agrees with them? How does your interaction change between those you agree with and those you don't?

TYPES OF LEADERS

I **HAVE ALWAYS BEEN** intrigued by the topic and study of leadership. It's such a vast field of differing theory, practice, tactics, characteristics, definitions and stories of triumph.

I like how there is no one right way to lead or to think of the body of knowledge that is leadership. But there is definitely a wrong way to lead. We've seen how that can result in detriment to the members of the group, whether it be the loss of power of the group, rebellion, or often times death in the case of nation-state and global affairs throughout history.

There are several different types of leaders and different personalities, approaches and ways of connecting.

Many respected thought influencers and leading academic thinkers on this topic have come to try and categorize different types of leaders into four main categories, and have found they often share traits and styles from two or more of these categories.

There are four main types:

1. Thought leaders
2. Courageous leaders
3. Inspirational leaders
4. Servant leaders[8]

THOUGHT LEADERS

Thought leaders are the intellectuals, those who harness their knowledge and innovative way of thinking about the world and the problems in front of them to find solutions and build.

They constantly push the envelope by showing how often contrarian viewpoints, theories or new technologies can reinvent old ways of doing things.

Think of Elon Musk or Steve Jobs, both visionary thought leaders who harnessed their understanding of their field's specific science to innovate beyond anyone's wildest imagination.

Jobs started a small computer hardware company and grew it through relentless thought and process, leadership and innovation, into what is now one of the most valuable companies in the world, with a tribe of loyal customers unlike any other company.

Musk is building an empire with Tesla, SpaceX and his other new ventures to tackle some of the world's most pressing and critical problems of this new century.

---

[8]   Paul B. Thornton, *Management Principles and Practices*, 5th ed. (WingSpan Press, 2013).

Both of these revolutionary business leaders also possess traits and styles from the category of inspirational leaders.

COURAGEOUS LEADERS

Courageous leaders bravely pursue a vision in the face of high risk, opposition and adversity.

They are driven by their "Why" and their convictions to change the world.

Think Lincoln, Martin Luther King, Jr., and other civil rights leaders. They take considerable personal and reputational risk in pursuit of a higher calling to move people to action and to bring meaningful change to the world.

INSPIRATIONAL LEADERS

Inspirational leaders advance and advocate change by the power of their unwavering commitment to their ideas, values and beliefs.

They have an innate ability to move people to look to the future, to what is beyond the present—to what is on the other side of fear—which we all know is greatness.

They are often skilled in language, rhetoric and persuasion.

They have an ability to connect with people at a deep and base level, appeal to their emotions and their "Why" and mobilize them to take action in pursuit of a common goal.

The first person that comes to mind in this category, for me, is Tony Robbins. He is a masterful, inspirational leader who has changed and positively affected hundreds of thousands of people's lives.

SERVANT LEADERS

Lastly we have Servant leaders, who care deeply about people and those they lead.

They seek to remove the social shackles and barriers that hold others back from achieving their full potential. They empower others by helping them, supporting and coaching them to their potential.

They have deep callings to change the lives of others for the better, and they are effective at doing so. Think of Mother Teresa, who dedicated her life to helping alleviate the world's biggest problem: poverty. Successful leaders generally fall into one of these categories or a combination of them.

There's no single leadership style that is best. We've seen there isn't only one right way to be a great and effective leader, one who can inspire and help others reach their potential, one who can help bring about change and progress to their group, organization, country or world.

What does remain true of all leaders, no matter their style and method of leading, is their desire to challenge the status quo and be bold.

LET'S GO!

POWER QUOTE

"If your actions inspire others to dream more, learn more, do more and become more, you are a leader."

—JOHN QUINCY ADAMS

KEY INSIGHT

All leaders, no matter their style and method of leading, have a desire to challenge the status quo and be bold.

TACTICAL TIP

Take a moment and find which leader categories you fit into, and look for other leaders who fall into those same styles. Look at the lives of those leaders in your categories, and learn from the examples of their lives.

DAY CHECK

Did you feel empowered today after reading about other leaders like you? Did you feel a new kind of strength after finding out what kind of leader you are? Did the knowledge of your leader categories help you help others better?

PART SEVEN

LEGACY

Your legacy is not defined by your achievements, but rather by the impact you have on people and the world.

YOUR LEGACY IS what you leave behind in the world when you are gone.

It is the summation of all of your actions, words, achievements, energies, contributions and feelings. It is the way in which you've influenced other people while on this earth. It is your impact for posterity, your contribution to the human experience and to humankind.

Unfortunately, most people do not live life with legacy front and center. People persist in jobs and careers they don't like or that do not give them joy and passion. They stay in relationships that are painful and mutually destructive. They go through life with a numbness and a routine regularity that breeds and sustains complacency, not inspiration.

However, we do not have to resign ourselves to this. We do not have to settle for this way of living and state of mind.

We have a chance each and every day to view that day as the beginning of the rest of our lives.

We have a unique opportunity to identify our purpose and define the legacy we want to leave for others in this world, and then develop a plan and put it into action each and every day so that we can live a life of impact, purpose and contribution.

Legacy for me is uniquely intertwined with my purpose and vision of positively impacting at least 100 million lives over the course of my lifetime.

I expect this vision to grow as my career and influence grows, but this is a good starting point. I have a lot of work ahead of me still!

When people that I love and care about talk about my life and my life's work at my funeral, I don't want to have any regrets. I want my legacy and reputation, my contribution to this thing we call life, to far outlast my very short and fleeting existence here in the flesh on this earth.

That's what *legacy* means to me and why it's so important to me. The following intentions and readings will help you find clarity on the legacy you want to leave and equip you with actionable tactics to work toward making this a reality.

GET THE FREE DOWNLOAD—*7 Frameworks to Live an Inspired Life—at LiveInspiredBook.com*

LEGACY

WHEN I LOST my father, it was very challenging to live the new normal without him.

He was such an amazing person in so many different ways, from the nature of his contribution, to the impact and effect he had on so many lives and in this world as a scholar, teacher and leader to others.

His legacy is one of lasting love, contribution, wisdom and overall greatness and completeness in life.

Legacy is defined in the dictionary as "something that is transmitted by or received from a predecessor or someone in the past to someone in the present."

Legacy can be thought of as a lasting reputation and impact that each of us has as individuals on the people that we encounter and interact with in life, and on our overall contribution to humanity and the human condition in a meaningful and positive way.

We often think about things that are very near-term or immediate—the things that we have to take care of today in this minute and hour—and sometimes we don't take the long view on life and legacy.

I would like you to spend thirty minutes sitting down and actually writing out your eulogy. What would be the ideal legacy that you would love and aspire to leave in this world if people other than yourself were to write about you and your life, and your impact on them and humanity?

This might not seem like a natural thing to do, and it might even be uncomfortable. I assure you, it will be very instructive and informative if you do it.

The reason why is that what we believe to be true, becomes true.

Putting our beliefs, reality and our vision down on paper and taking deliberate and consistent action toward achieving them is hugely powerful.

The mere act of doing this will start to program your subconscious mind and psyche to move toward accomplishing those things that you hope to be remembered for.

So take twenty or thirty minutes and do this exercise in a very open, honest and transparent way with yourself.

What does your legacy look like?

Who are the people you have touched and impacted in a positive and transformative way?

What does your family look like, and how do they remember you?

For what values are you known?

What causes were important to you philanthropically?

How successful were you in business relationships, financially and in other important and major areas of your life?

What are the things that you hope your family and friends will remember most about you?

I assure you, doing this will be powerful for you.

LET'S GO!

 ## POWER QUOTE

"Please think about your legacy, because you're writing it every day."

—GARY VAYNERCHUK

 ## KEY INSIGHT

Putting our beliefs, reality and our vision down on paper and taking deliberate and consistent action toward achieving them is hugely powerful. The mere act of doing this will start to program your subconscious mind and psyche to move toward accomplishing those things that you hope to be remembered for.

TACTICAL TIP

How do you want to be remembered, and what will your legacy be? Write out your eulogy and see how powerful it can be.

DAY CHECK

What are some things you did today that will contribute to your legacy?

PLAN TO GROW

WHEN ANY YEAR winds down, there's often a lot of talk about finishing strong, but it is just as important to set ourselves up to have a stronger year next year.

When we do this and plan properly, it takes a lot of time, effort and diligence in reviewing our performance and reports.

It requires stepping back and elevating up to a hundred, a thousand, ten thousand feet above our lives and our businesses to really evaluate where we are and the progress we have made this year regarding our goals.

It also gives us a chance to review and see what is working and what isn't, where we can put more emphasis and move more resources toward our strengths, and do the same in areas that could use improvement.

Personally I'm a big fan of really knowing yourself and knowing what our strengths are, what our drivers are and what our main levers of influence are. That way we can refine, build and grow those in the areas we need, admitting and understanding that it's okay to not be good at everything.

It's okay to not be as great at something as we might like, but know that somebody else is probably far better skilled and a better fit to do certain things that we might not like to do, do well or want to do.

I went down to Philadelphia to attend an intensive event that's put on by one of the best public speaking and performance leaders in the country.

The reason I went is not because I don't know anything about public speaking, or don't have a skill set in public speaking, or want to get into public speaking.

No—rather contrary to all of those, as public speaking is a key part of what I do in my business and in my personal life, I identified that I really want to grow this skill even further and take it to the next level.

I wanted to build on my strengths and find ways to reach more people, be more effective, be influential in my communications and in the way in which I interact with others.

These things will ultimately help me in all of my professional areas of pursuit as well as in relationships and in my personal life.

So today I want to ask and challenge you to identify a couple of skills and things that you are both really good at and that you like doing.

Then think about the last time you actually invested time and money in improving this skill.

Whether it's working with a coach, attending an event, doing some other professional group work or anything else, you need to very intentionally work on putting the accelerator down on advancing and getting better in that key area of strength.

Then I want you to do some research and find out ways you can take that skill to the next level and really find the edge and see how that can advance your business and your life in significant ways.

Continue to refine, enhance and grow in areas where you're already strong and have talent, versus focusing on areas of improvement where you're not strong to begin with.

One of the things I sometimes hear but disagree with is that we are generally taught and shown that we need to be investing in our areas of weakness, or maybe we need help improving in some categories.

I'm going to take the contrarian viewpoint against conventional wisdom and say outside of those three to five key skills and strengths anyone might have, the rest should be handed off and delegated to other people that are better at and more interested in doing those things.

Do that instead of spending all the time, valuable effort and focus to try to get those skills up to just a minor passing grade or satisfactory level of proficiency.

Let's know what we're good at and know what we're not—and be okay with it.

So let's take some time today and identify key areas and skills where we can really push it.

Look to build on those inherent strengths and skills that each of us possesses as part of our unique offering to the world.

LET'S GO!

 ## POWER QUOTE

"Strength and growth come only through continuous effort and struggle."

—NAPOLEON HILL

 ## KEY INSIGHT

I'm going to take the contrarian viewpoint against conventional wisdom and say outside of those three to five key skills and strengths anyone might have, the rest should be handed off and delegated to other people that are better at and more interested in doing those things, versus spending all the time and valuable effort and focus to try to get those skills up to just a minor passing grade or satisfactory level of proficiency.

TACTICAL TIP

Take a moment and write down three to five core strengths you have. What are ways you can enhance those strengths?

 ## DAY CHECK

Did you delegate things to people who are better than you in that area? Did you notice how you let others handle stuff you were not equipped to handle and moved on to what you could do?

INTENTION 54

DAY ONE

ONE OF OUR panels at a recent event focused on talking about culture and company philosophy and how this can make or break an organization.

This has been a perennial favorite of mine, and I've spoken on it several times. Culture is so critical, and one of my favorite business activities to focus on is improving and innovating.

The example that was used to deliver the message concerning the importance of culture was that of Amazon and their extraordinary culture, foundational values and principles.

Amazon continues to innovate, accelerate and dominate in the markets they compete in—which is basically anything that can be sold online.

Which is a lot!

There are a lot of reasons for this, and I read and loved the book *The Amazon Way* and the fourteen leadership principles that have underpinned their success to better understand their achievements.

In my early research and in following this extraordinary company, what I've seen is that a lot of it can be attributed to a very simple principle and belief:

Every day is Day 1 at Amazon.

Jeff Bezos has made the idea that it's always "Day 1" at the company—a leading mantra meant to convey that the company will never stop being a start-up, never become complacent, never stop innovating and never stop putting their customer first, above all else. In a letter to shareholders in 2016 that's been widely publicized and broadcast, Bezos was quoted saying:

Day 2 is stasis. Followed by irrelevance. Followed by excruciating, painful decline. Followed by death," he said. *"And that is why it is always Day 1.*[9]

Leaders at Amazon start with the customer and work backwards. This is not always the natural thought process or pattern of management and leadership.

I know I don't always start with what a potential client needs or what their potential pain points might be.

I try to, but I sometimes go for building value and discussing my team's unique approach first and then ask questions—instead of trying to understand their situation and needs and wants by putting myself in their shoes first.

Bezos has stated that a company can be centered on many things, including products, technology, business model and more, but that the best way to protect what he called "Day 1 Vitality" is to be obsessively focused on customers.

---

[9]   Jeff Bezos (Founder and Chief Executive Officer, Amazon.com, Inc.), 2016 Letter to Shareholders, https://www.sec.gov/Archives/edgar/data/1018724/000119312517120198/d373368dex991.htm.

He explained that customers can keep you on track because "customers are always beautifully, wonderfully dissatisfied, even when they report being happy and business is great.

The customer, he added, "Always wants something better, and focusing on not just keeping people happy, but delighting them, drives innovation."

I think we can all benefit by taking serious heed to this idea of placing the customer first, whether that's a buyer or a seller, or if you're in another industry.

Let's make a collective effort to leave the ego out of it, leave our teams, companies and greatness and the most amazing value proposition you've ever heard—out of it.

Let's be the best listeners we've ever been.

Let's ask the thoughtful and tough questions of our customers. Let's drive and dig to uncover their deepest fears and concerns, and identify what they're truly seeking.

Only then will we be able to tailor our approach and deliver exceedingly high levels of value in both products, but more importantly, the service we give them. When we do this, we create trust, we create loyalty and we create customers and clients for life.

So, let's be mindful of how we interact with our customers today and this week and attempt to implement this ideology and foundational principle.

Let's go into those conversations with our team members and our business partners as if it's "Day 1" and we are just starting out.

Everything we do has a direct effect on whether we succeed or fail. Let's refuse to become complacent no matter how successful we become.

Let's place innovation and an unending and unwavering commitment to growth and to never being content with the status quo at the top of our priorities.

Let's create a culture in our professional lives that is centered on the philosophy of "Day 1," a culture where we have never been more hungry, eager, committed, conscientious and more determined to continue to grow, lead and contribute to others.

Just like when we started on that energy-filled day of vision and hope that is known as "Day 1."

LET'S GO!

 POWER QUOTE

"Day 2 is stasis. Followed by irrelevance. Followed by excruciating, painful decline. Followed by death. And that is why it is always Day 1."

—JEFF BEZOS

KEY INSIGHT

Everything we do has a direct effect on whether we succeed or fail. Let's refuse to become complacent no matter how successful we become. Let's place innovation and an unending and unwavering commitment to growth and to never being content with the status quo at the top of our priorities.

 ## TACTICAL TIP

When you're brainstorming ways to get a product out or sell a service, think about the audience you are serving. Instead of focusing on your needs, focus on your customers' needs, then see how those needs line up with yours.

 ## DAY CHECK

How did thinking about the customer first change your mindset? Did you notice how thinking of your target audience gave you more peace of mind than when you focused on your own needs?

THINK AHEAD

WHEN WE LOOK at each year's goals, I suggest that we all take some additional time to look at what our goals are for the next two, three and five years.

What does our team or practice look like then? Does it require additional team members to achieve those goals? What type of people will be critical to execution? What systems and resources will we have to develop to achieve these goals and this growth?

Now I want you to fast-forward the timetable for all of this growth, meaning why will it take you a year to hire two more people? What are you waiting for?

Why not hire them both in the next three months, and future pace your growth by fast-charging your support systems to handle them?

That new lead source system that's been hanging around your "do, doing, done board" for the past six months—let's get it implemented ASAP.

We need to not let up on what it takes to grow our market share, and take business from our competitors.

We should be less worried about our direct-cost increases to attain this new business, and even ok with smaller margins as we scale and grow our market share in key markets. We should be focused on growth and attraction of the right talent to grow our teams and practice.

Jeff Bezos is famous for not turning a profit at Amazon for years, and being less concerned with margins than he is with market share in any market they choose to compete in.

Free cash flows and gains over competitors are important, and when he wins customer loyalty and controls a market, the margins will then increase over time through that dominant position and through economies of scale.

Specifically, Amazon and Bezos' approach should inspire companies to do business the way Amazon does—sacrificing this year's profits to invest in long-term customer loyalty and product opportunities that will create bigger profits next year and for years thereafter.

The way most companies do business is to focus primarily on today's bottom line.

The prevailing ethos in corporate America, after all, is that companies exist to make money for their owners—and the more and the sooner, the better—so every decision should be made in the context of that.[10]

---

[10]   Henry Blodget, "Amazon's Letter To Shareholders Should Inspire Every Company In America," *Business Insider*, April 14, 2019, Accessed December 5, 2019, https://www.businessinsider.com/amazons-letter-to-shareholders-2013-4

If we are going to continue to grow and outgrow our competitors, we must future-pace and over-invest even a bit beyond our comfort zones to fast-track this growth. I mean invest in those systems, people and marketing spending before you had planned to or thought it was justified.

Let's be confident in our business and in our value proposition to clients, and put our money where our mouth is.

Let's invest-up in that new system, that higher level of coaching, that new team member that looks to be a star...even before we think we can justify it.

Let's believe in ourselves and in our story of growth enough to do it now, betting on ourselves and our future.

Let's future pace and grow into the business and world we create—by design, starting today.

LET'S GO!

 POWER QUOTE

"If you invest the time earlier to create structure and process around communication, planning, and goal-setting, you can prevent missteps before they occur."

—CHRISTINE TSAI

KEY INSIGHT

We should be less worried about our direct-cost increases to attain this new business, and even ok with smaller margins as we scale and grow our market share in key markets. We should be focused on growth and attraction of the right talent to grow our teams and practice.

 ## TACTICAL TIP

What do you need to grow your business? What are your waiting for? How can you grow your audience? Think about these questions, and similar ones. You need to make sure you have the resources before you grow your audience.

 ## DAY CHECK

In what ways did you stop stalling today? What did you do today that you have been putting off?

INTENTION 56

BUILD A TEAM

I WANT TO FOCUS on giving everybody some tangible, actionable strategies and steps to really kick their professional and personal lives into high gear in every major category and sense.

What I want to suggest to you today is to encourage the development of the business-owner mindset, not just the top-producer mindset in your chosen career and line of work. If you're coming from the business-owner mindset and perspective, you are focused on owning a system, not a job.

I'm spending a lot of time and capital to build out a repeatable system where I can hire people to perform the different functions while I lead and manage. Not while I produce.

The reason is this: what happens if I get sick, want to go an extended vacation, or want to do other things with my other businesses?

The answer is, if I own a job, my income and business grind to a halt. What happens if I want to sell my client book of business and my team down the road, but I'm producing the majority of the sales, and clients in the market have come to expect me and working directly with me when they call my team?

The answer is, I won't be able to sell my team very easily at all.

What happens, however, if I have a well-oiled machine with various systems and repeatable processes that produce reliable and predictable results for our clients with consistent service and accuracy?

Now, all of a sudden, I'm the owner of a system, not a job. And the owner of a system can sell that system for a multiple of earnings anywhere between three- and maybe five-times, depending on a few other factors.

Consider forming a team once you get to a certain level of production as a next step in your growth, to further leverage and build the business owner mindset and exit strategy into your company, and evolve from the self-employed mindset and strategy.

Watch how you can use these principles to change your entire way of thinking and how you approach business and wealth creation.

It will open up many doors and allow you to start to enter the next mindset shift and evolution, which is to that of an investor.

LET'S GO!

 POWER QUOTE

"Delegating doesn't mean passing off work you don't enjoy, but letting your employees stretch their skills and judgment."

—HARVEY MACKAY

KEY INSIGHT

What I would encourage everyone to do—and even if you don't run a team this can still apply to you—is work toward systematizing everything in your job or business and embrace the concept of leverage, leverage of your time and your capital and resources.

TACTICAL TIP

Take some time and think about what you do for your business or company. Are you the main producer? What are ways that you can step down so that others can grow and not rely on you as much?

DAY CHECK

In what way today did you step down and let someone else grow? Did you notice how it felt to release control?

CONCLUSION

Y OU MADE IT! But the journey really begins now, with a unique opportunity that lies in front of you: Right now, in this very moment, this instant—you have a choice.

How you are going to live the rest of your life?

How you are going to show up every day?

You deserve to truly live an Inspired Life—to seize control of your destiny, be more mindful, intentional, and energized in every area of your life!

In order to do that, however, you have to ask the hard questions of yourself and others.

You have to be open and honest about yourself and the world around you.

You have to value and seek the truth at whatever cost and place the need for radical honesty and transparency foremost in all of your endeavors.

To live inspired, you have to stay energized. You have to stay committed with the clarity and the necessity of your vision.

You must chase your vision and goals with extreme commitment.

I found success in life by maintaining my commitment to my vision, and to constant growth and development each day.

Now it's your turn to do the same.

You're not alone though. Let's take this journey together. I'm here to support you in your walk.

Are you ready?

Then...

Let's GO!

Keir Weimer

ACKNOWLEDGEMENTS

THERE ARE FAR too many people to list individually here who've had some positive influence on me and contributed to my growth and development as a person—and to this project in particular.

I believe no one is really "self-made," achieves happiness and success in life on his or her own, or does much of anything without the influence, support and help of others. From family members, friends, colleagues, business partners, communities, society and this great country of America, we are all a unique function of the collection of our backgrounds, environments and experiences.

With that said, without the support and help of a few key people, I wouldn't be where I am today. And I certainly wouldn't have put this book together and carried it out into the world.

I want to thank my Father and my Mother, Mark Weimer and Gail Doering, for their unwavering and absolute support, and for their unending love for me through thick and thin, from beginning to end. I want to thank my late father, Mark, for dedicating his life to his two boys and their happiness and success. My father was a beacon of strength for me, throughout life and through my darkest times. He was and remains my best friend. From attending every varsity basketball game two hours away after a long day of work, to visiting me every weekend while I was away at my lowest point, to editing and scanning the manuscript for the stories I would mail home from prison after writing them on my typewriter for my first book—my dad never gave up on me. In turn, he taught me to never give up on myself. I miss you more than you know, Dad, but feel you still with me every step of the way.

I want to thank my mother, Gail Doering, who has been more than just the best mother I could ever imagine or ask for. You have also been a true best friend, a leader to me and a shining example of what love and life really should be about. Your grace, generosity, kindness and wit are appreciated beyond description. I love and respect you more than you'll ever know. Thank you for always supporting me and believing in me.

I want to thank my younger brother, Jared, for being the best little brother I could ever ask for. You've been there through the hardest of times. I am so grateful for the great friendship and relationship we've developed over the years. I'm thrilled to see you continue to grow and develop as a father, son, brother, friend and a positive example and role model for so many people.

I would like to thank my amazing team at my multimedia company for their support and help in putting this project together. Thank you to all of our partners in business who've also contributed to this project directly and indirectly. These include but are not limited to: Storybuilders, Brand Builders Group, Bullen Publishing Services and BrandMagic LA.

Thank you to all of my friends, colleagues, partners and supporters—far too many to list—who have been there and supported me—and continue to be there—throughout this amazing journey. I truly feel like we are only just getting started!

Thank you, from the bottom of my heart.
Keir

ABOUT THE AUTHOR

K**EIR WEIMER IS** an internationally recognized real estate and lifestyle entrepreneur. Having started and grown multiple businesses, Keir has a passion for entrepreneurship and novel ideas.

Before his success, however, Keir spent almost four years in prison as a result of an accident he caused that claimed the life of his friend in college. This experience galvanized his determination to live a life of purpose and contribution in pursuit of redemption.

By developing an extreme commitment to his vision, Keir has been able to persevere through the challenges and obstacles he's encountered. As a result, he's built a life of purpose, abundance and happiness. Keir loves helping others grow and live a life of freedom on their terms as well.

As an internationally-recognized, luxury real estate & lifestyle entrepreneur who has been featured in major global media outlets such as the *Wall Street Journal, The New York Times, Bloomberg* and *Sotheby's International Realty*, Keir is now focused on sharing his expertise and wisdom through a next-generation education and information company, Keir Weimer Multimedia, LLC. When Keir isn't working on the next big idea or venture, you can find him traveling the world, exploring new places and cultures and enjoying the outdoors.

To connect directly with Keir, visit his website: **KeirWeimer.com**. You can find his blog there and receive updates on new content, resources and announcements.

You can also follow Keir on Facebook and Instagram or find him on LinkedIn by searching "Keir Weimer".

FREE RESOURCES — To get free access to the digital resources and worksheets referenced throughout this book, please visit: **LiveInspiredBook.com**